# FORK in the ROAD

D1545575

## STORIES
## FROM THE FILES OF
## PURE LIFE MINISTRIES

# STEVE GALLAGHER

ISBN   0-9702202-4-3

Copies of this book or other materials
which help men come out of habitual
sexual sin, may be obtained through:

## Pure Life Ministries

P.O. Box 410
Dry Ridge, KY 41035
(800) 635-1866
(859) 824-4444
(859) 824-5159 FAX
*www.purelifeministries.org*

Unless otherwise noted, Scripture taken from the NEW AMERICAN
STANDARD BIBLE, ©Copyright 1960, 1962, 1963, 1968, 1971, 1972, 1973,
1975, 1977, 1988, The Lockman Foundation. Used by permission.

## Author's Note

Some names have been changed and events slightly altered at the author's discretion to protect the intimate details of the lives of certain individuals. An asterick is provided by those names and stories which have been altered.

Although the author was personally mentioned in some of the stories, they were written from a third person point of view.

## Acknowledgements

To Kevin Teachey for the wonderful ideas he shared for each story,
and
To Bradley Furges--where would I be without his editorial skills?

*To the Staff of Pure Life Ministries*
*Who lay their lives down daily*
*In a very difficult ministry*
*For people who often don't see it.*

# Table of Contents

# Introduction

"It is still 'either-or.' If we insist on keeping Hell (or even earth) we shall not see Heaven: if we accept Heaven we shall not be able to retain even the smallest and most inimate souvenirs of Hell."

C.S. Lewis

When I am at home, every morning is virtually the same. I spend my first hour, coffee in hand, studying the Bible. Then I spend the next hour going on my prayer walk. After breakfast, our staff spends another hour praying for different needs. In contrast, when I am out on the road travelling, my prayer walks are often in less than desirable places: shopping center parking lots, cemeteries, or, if I'm fortunate, a quiet field with a trail through it. So, while at home, I greatly appreciate my "prayer trail."

I begin my walk by circling around the top of the ridge before making my way down the meandering trail to the creek. I walk along the creek bed until I come to the northwest corner of the property, where I begin the long ascent back up to the top of the ridge. It is at this northwest corner of the property that I come to a fork in the trail. When Bart, our shih tzu dog, gets there ahead of me, he stops to see which way I will go. In his little mind, he does not understand that it is the wetness of the ground that determines the direction. I prefer to stay on the main trail which winds its way through the trees along the north side of the property, slowly making its way up to the top of the hill. However, if it has rained, the trail becomes muddy and on those mornings I cut up the grassy hillside which is a much steeper climb.

Most people who are on the Christian journey will eventually come to a fork in the road: a place where they will be forced to make a major life-decision. For many, it will prove to be the defining moment of their Christian existence. Which path they choose to take will, to a large extent, determine how the rest of their lives will unfold, and what will await them in eternity. Not only will their own lives be affected by the decision, but their loved ones also will be influenced and affected. Depending on the choice, those closest to the individual will often either be tremendously blessed or completely destroyed.

It is a matter of fact that Christians face many forks in the road. Throughout our lives we make a million small, daily choices which establish a pattern of life. However, this book contains true stories about individuals who were confronted with that one major, life-defining moment which greatly impacted the remainder of their lives.

The Bible is replete with stories of forced decisions.* Jesus called on those who would be His followers to make the hard decisions which would bring them into intimacy with Him. Just one of many was the rich young ruler who approached Him to find out the requirements to receive eternal life. Jesus told him to keep the commandments. His response indicated his insincerity when he said that he had kept them since childhood. Jesus, looking right into his heart said, "One thing you lack: go and sell all you possess, and give to the poor, and you shall have treasure in heaven; and come, follow Me." This was a pivotal moment for this young man. Would he surrender his idol of possessions to be a follower of Jesus, or would he continue on down the same path of dead religion he had maintained thus far? "But at these words his face fell, and he went away grieved, for he was one who owned much property," is all that Mark tells us. He made his decision. He preferred to maintain a facade of spirituality, while in reality only serving himself.

Jesus faced a fork in the road Himself at Gethsamane. Facing

---

* For a sobering study about the consequences of our choices, meditate on and pray over the verses containing the word <u>if</u> which are located in the addendum on page 107.

the most horrible death, and worse, taking onto His innocent soul every filthy and vile sin committed by man, He was forced to decide if He would avoid or embrace what God had chosen for Him. Perhaps this is what the writer of Hebrews had in mind when he established the course of real Christianity:

> Wherefore seeing we also are compassed about with so great a cloud of witnesses, let us lay aside every weight, and the sin which doth so easily beset us, and let us run with patience the race that is set before us, Looking unto Jesus the author and finisher of our faith; who for the joy that was set before him endured the cross, despising the shame, and is set down at the right hand of the throne of God. (Hebrews 12:1-2 KJV)

This passage of Scripture, which makes mention of the great decision Jesus had to make, reveals that the fork in the road experience is there to give the person the opportunity to give something up for the sake of God. It might be some besetting sin like pride, sexual perversion, or covetousness. Or it might be the weight of some idol such as possessions, loved ones, or a career. Whatever it is that is faced, the situation has been created to force the person to make a choice about whether he will keep the object of affection or whether he will relinquish it and do what is pleasing to God. All the while, Jesus is standing where the road forks into two, bidding the traveller to enter the narrow path--the higher calling which is a the life of surrender.

If the man accepts the challenge and enters that narrow path, all weights must come off and be left behind. It is almost always a very painful forfeiture. A loss is involved. Something which has been valued is required of the person. Some simply cannot bear the loss. It is too overwhelming. The person cannot imagine life without it.

However, some will choose to make the hard decision, knowing they must obey God whatever the cost. It is sometimes an excruciating extraction, as the sin or idol is ripped from the person's breast and thrown down on the roadside. Nevertheless, to the person's utter amazement, he finds that once the detrimental baggage has been shed, there is a freedom experienced he had never known. In spite of the fact that he may still be mourning over the loss, he feels as light as a feather! He simply did not realize what a heavy burden he was carrying around. God forces the decision not to make His child miserable, but to set him free!

The other aspect to it is that, just like air rushes into fill a vacuum, so too does the Holy Spirit quickly take possession of every vacated room in a person's heart. Once self has been driven out of that particular area, it is open territory for the Lord to fill. The person who steps through the narrow gate soon discovers that his capacity to be filled with Jesus has been enlarged. Many small choices for the Lord will do the same thing, but there is something special which occurs for the person who makes that great sacrifice, that deep surrender, or that profound repentance. Something in him has been conquered by God.

Decisions like these tend to occur in greater frequency and intensity where the presence of God is felt more strongly. This is why real revivals result in many people making a decision to follow Christ. The presence of God appears and people are then forced to decide if they are going to be Christians or if they are going to blatantly refuse to follow the Lord. Charles Finney was known to enter the sleepiest "Christian" towns and bring such a fire from God that people would literally fall over from the Lord's presence. Jonathan Edwards, a Calvinist who preached during the Great Awakening, was known to preach with a dull, monotone voice, and yet people would clutch the pews feeling as though the ground were opening up beneath them and they were sliding into hell itself.

Pure Life Ministries is not a place of revival, nor is it a ministry with an evangelistic thrust. Our call is to help (presumably Christian) men come out of habitual sexual sin. However, the presence of God can often be felt in a very strong way at the facility, whether in our meetings, in private devotions, or even in a counseling session. When His presence is felt in a strong way, people find themselves being dealt with by God. The inevitable crisis is encountered, the decision forced, and the destiny thereby determined. Many, many times I have witnessed men (and their visiting wives) come face-to-face with the Lord, only to be forced to decide if they truly are serious about following Him or not.

Such decision-making is what this book is about. The purpose is to help the reader, who may never come to PLM, learn from the decisions others have made. Perhaps God will put His finger on something in your heart which stands in the way of the intimacy He longs to have with you. Maybe this book will bring about a fork in your road that will allow you to know the glories of the higher, more narrow path of genuine Christianity. One thing the reader can be assured of: the greater the loss, the more wonderful the blessing will be on the other side of it.

Each of the stories shared in this small book are unique. I have presented the reader with a variety of situations which will hopefully offer a wide perspective of the way God deals with people. Some of these stories are wonderful testimonies of how the Lord changes lives from the inside-out. Others are more tragic and have been very painful to write about. Each story which tells of a poor choice represents a great deal of personal heartache. When you have spent months or years pouring yourself into someone, teaching him, counseling him, talking with him, encouraging him, rebuking him, and most of all, spending countless hours pleading on his behalf at the Throne of Grace, how can words describe the loss one feels when that person turns away from the Savior? As much as it may pain me to write about these heart-rending stories, in the end, I felt that these, in particular must be told.

Many of the stories have been written about those who have been or are currently on staff with Pure Life Ministries. One reason for this is simply that I am much more intimately aware of the details of their lives. But there is another reason beyond that. When one sets himself on a course of coming into a deeper intimacy with God-- which is the case with anybody who is invited to come on staff at PLM--the issues they face are often deeply buried and enormous in influence. Some of these people had wonderful breakthroughs in the live-in program only to face deeper issues while on staff that forced them to make a much greater consecration to God.

All of it has been written with the reader in mind. I hope that these stories challenge you to respond in the affirmative when the Lord moves in and brings you to your own *Fork In The Road.*

# 1

## From Bronx to Broadway

"Behold, the eye of the LORD is on those who fear Him, on those who hope for His lovingkindness."

the Psalmist

In the early '80s, Paul Newman played a tough street cop in a movie entitled, "Fort Apache." The film was named after a rough neighborhood in the South Bronx. Much of the movie was filmed on location, deep in the heart of one of the most violent areas in the world. After the day's shoot, Newman, no doubt, would find his way to a posh hotel somewhere in Manhattan.

But for a little black Puerto Rican kid named Kamal Sabir, Fort Apache was home. There was no escaping the overwhelming sense of hopelessness that hovered like a cloud of foreboding darkness over the area. There was no getting away from the constant sense of fear. He never knew when older kids, or perhaps a gang, would attack him. He never knew when guns would be drawn and bullets would fly in front of the bar on the corner. Growing up in such a precarious environment was all that Kamal had ever been exposed to--this was his life.

One would like to think that a little kid forced to live under such harsh circumstances would be sheltered from it in a loving, nurturing home, where his parents would know the value of establishing an atmosphere which fostered stability and security in a youngster's life. But such was not the case for little Kamal. His chaotic home was dominated by the strong presence of his grandmother, who he was raised to believe was his mother. A controlling, schizophrenic woman, she set the tone which fostered a lot of bickering, backbiting, and even violence. Her husband, who went off the deep-end after killing someone years before, was a heavy alcoholic who could no longer control himself, often shaking and wetting himself.

When he was eleven-years old, Kamal's "oldest sister," a street prostitute with a deadly heroin addiction, informed him that she was actually his mother. This news devastated him, shattering what little security he had in life. From then on, life seemed more and more confusing and unpredictable. Nor were things any better for him at school. The teachers working in his ghetto school were hard and uncaring. One day, while in the fifth grade, Kamal was talking to another kid in class when his teacher came up behind him and thumped him in the head with his knuckles. Kamal quickly retaliated, throwing a book and hitting the man in the face. He was suspended from school and rarely went back after that incident.

It was in 1970, at the age of thirteen, that this troubled boy first smoked marijuana. A few months later, he joined the Royal Knights, a predominantly black street gang. He was a member of the gang for about a year, but not being one too particularly drawn to street violence, his devotion to the gang began to drift away. One day, a friend began teaching him how to play the drums. Kamal was a natural. He could play for hours, escaping into his own little world where there was no fear and no rejection. No one could hurt him there; he was safe and he was in control. Before long, he joined a band playing soul music in bars, clubs, dance halls and block parties. At fourteen years of age, he played in the Celebrity Club, one of the most prestigious black nightclubs in the country.

About that time, his grandmother's husband died of liver

failure. When this happened, his grandmother decided to move back to Puerto Rico. Kamal considered himself to be a black American and had no interest in his Hispanic roots. He refused to go with her and was left to fend for himself on the streets. Many nights he would sleep on the subway which travelled over to Coney Island and back, sometimes waking up to a car full of early morning commuters staring at him. Most of the time, however, he slept in the basement of a tenement building located nearby. As difficult as life was on the streets, anything was a welcome relief from living in the turbulent home he had grown up in.

Playing in the band gave Kamal a purpose in life--a sense of belonging. This was his only outlet. When he was fifteen, a music teacher befriended him and began to take a real interest in him. Kamal was excited to learn how to read music, how to make the most of his abilities. Most of all, the mere fact that someone really cared for him was a wonderful, new sensation to him. It wasn't long before he would come to realize that such affection had a price tag attached to it. The teacher was a homosexual pedophile who took advantage of the vulnerable young teen by seducing him into having sex with him. The troubled teen was not homosexually inclined, but was willing to be involved in return for food, a warm bed, and the musical instruction he received. It was in the molester's home that Kamal was first exposed to the dark, seedy world of pornography.

One day, while his band was rehearsing, three young black men showed up to watch them play. It was an up-and-coming singing trio called the Delphonics. They liked what they heard and hired Kamal and his friends to play as their back-up band. The teenagers were astounded--they were in the "big league" now! Over the next couple of years they played in all the hottest clubs in New York. It wasn't uncommon for them to share the stage with singers like Al Green and groups like the Temptations or Cool and the Gang. Kamal was regularly backstage with the stars of the black music industry.

Life was beginning to deal this young man a decent hand for a change. It wasn't long before he got a small apartment--all to himself--near the Rockefeller Center in Manhattan. He was having the time of his life, dating beautiful girls, snorting cocaine, and partying with popular entertainers.

One night in 1975, Kamal stopped by to see his mother who

was staying in a dumpy hotel in Manhattan. She had abandoned her life of prostitution by this time, but was still using heroin. He would actually smoke marijuana with her on occasion, maintaining some semblance of a relationship with the woman who had given him physical life, but so little else. One evening he was visiting, she was so drugged that she couldn't even feel the lit cigarette burning into the flesh of her chest where it had fallen. She eventually "nodded out" and he went home. He was a little concerned about her the next morning so he called the hotel, asking for her room number.

"The body is in the room," came the monotone answer from the front-desk clerk who had long since grown accustomed to such events.

Staggering at the words, Kamal yelled back, "What are you talking about?"

"The woman in that room died last night," came the slightly irritated response. "I hear she overdosed." Later that day, Kamal was called to Bellevue Hospital. He was led to a small window by an orderly who had the same calloused attitude Kamal had grown so accustomed to in New York life: "Please step up to the window and tell me if you recognize the person." With a pounding heart, he stepped forward hesitantly, afraid of what he would see. The body was covered in a black bag with only the woman's head protruding from the end uncovered. The head was swollen--a mere caricature of his mother. But there was no mistaking the face he had once known as only his sister's. "It's my mother," he said, all his energy seeming to drain from his body as he stood there.

Kamal handled this blow as he had learned to handle all disappointments in life: by throwing himself into his music and into his increasing obsession with sex and drugs. He had become well-known in the black music world of New York and could land a job anywhere. Pretty soon, he was playing with ensembles and small orchestras in off-Broadway productions. Then, he got another break when he landed the job of drummer for Cab Calloway's Broadway musical, "Bubbling Brown Sugar." He now began travelling outside of New York, where there was an entire world he knew nothing about!

In 1981, at the age of twenty-four, he was hired to play in Roberta Flack's band. They travelled all over America and even to the Middle East. This was really the big time, staying in the finest hotels and arriving at concerts in chauffeured limousines. He didn't even have to set up his own drums, a road crew did everything for them!

For the next several years, Kamal broadened his horizons by playing more and more with jazz bands such as Ornnett Coleman's. By this time, even though he was making big money, every bit of it was needed to pay for his growing cocaine addiction. He began borrowing money from other musicians, running up huge debts with his friends. As the addiction mounted, he also started ducking out of concerts during the breaks to get high, many times leaving the bewildered band to finish the set without a drummer. He simply failed to show up altogether at numerous other shows.

Kamal Sabir was in deep trouble. He tried going to therapy, reading self-help books, even turning to new age teachings in his quest for the fulfillment in life that eluded him. On Halloween night in 1987, he ran into a girl he had known from his schoolyard days who had become a Christian. She told him that the Lord could help him through a ministry called Teen Challenge in Brooklyn. That very night he took a subway to the center which had become famous some years earlier through the book *The Cross and the Switchblade*. He pounded on the door, demanding to be admitted. It was 4:30 in the morning and they told him to go away. They finally opened the door when they saw how persistent he was.

For the next eighteen months, Kamal stayed within the confines of Teen Challenge. The first few months were spent there in Brooklyn, but later he was transferred to a Teen Challenge Center in Brockton, Massachusetts. One Sunday evening, as he was preparing to graduate, an evangelist preached at the Assembly of God church where the men in the program regularly attended. It was a fiery preacher named Steve Gallagher, who shared his testimony about how he had been set free from *sexual addiction*. This concept fascinated Kamal who approached him after the meeting. Kamal had been freed from his drug addiction but continued to struggle privately with masturbation and sexual fantasy.

It was a brief conversation, but a few years later, as he continued to struggle, Kamal contacted Pure Life Ministries, seeking further help. In September of 1994, he enrolled in the live-in program. Although the Teen Challenge program had played a major role in his life, establishing God's authority and learning self-discipline, the deeper issues of his heart had not yet been dealt with. Kamal recounts his early days at PLM:

One of the first things the Lord began to deal with me about at Pure Life was a deep-seated attitude that I was a victim in life and, therefore, was not to be held responsible for my behavior. Somewhere along the line, I had come to understand what a poor upbringing I had. I began to see myself as a victim. Self-pity became an excuse for anything I wanted to do. It kept me from accepting responsibility for my actions in life. While I was at Pure Life, God made it very real to me that I was no longer a victim, but had, in fact, become a victimizer. I was destroying lives, just as others had done to me. I used other people without any concern for them whatsoever. The only person I cared about was myself. The picture God showed me of what I was really like was horrible. I knew I needed to change.

The Lord also began to show me how I had created a false image of Him. I seemed to vacillate between one extreme to the other. One day I saw Him as a loving God, but I just used this as an excuse to give over to my sin. "If He's so full of grace, surely He understands my struggles." Then, the next day, after I had plunged myself into sin again, I would make Him out to be an angry, vengeful tyrant who was looking to pour out His wrath on me. I could never seem to find the right balance.

I could see that the leaders at Pure Life had a fresh and real experience with God. It showed in their lives. I started to realize that God was not the angry tyrant I had made Him out to be. He was not sick-and-tired of me and my failures. He really did love me and desperately wanted to help me. I saw the gravity and ugliness of my sin and how flippant I had been about it in the past. Yes, God loved me greatly, that I came to understand, but what also became very real to me at PLM was that God is not mocked.

I came to a crossroads where I had to decide if I was going to repent of my selfish lifestyle and live the mercy to others that God had shown me, or would I retreat back into my self-pity and refuse to face what I was like. My time at Pure Life was the hardest time of my life. There were times the pain seemed unbearable, but I couldn't go on being a hypocrite. In the end, I knew what I saw there was real and I had to face the music. If I didn't respond to God I would end up dying.

Kamal graduated the program in the spring of 1995 and went to work for the ministry in the office. He continued to live there for another eighteen months as God cemented into him the truths that he had learned. In 1996, he began sensing that it was time to move on. He moved back up to the Boston area and began working in a state-funded home for troubled children. It was a wonderful opportunity for him to pour into others the love which God had lavished on him.

In the fall of 1999, the Gallaghers visited with Kamal and his new wife. They could hardly believe it was the same troubled man who had gone through the live-in program! He had always seemed so fragile inside, but now there was a solidness in his character that was not there before. Something was completely different. He had "faced his demons" and now had a new life to show for it.

Kamal is doing drum demonstrations these days in secular high schools, where he is able to share his testimony about how God took him out of the darkest pit and brought him into the light. Yes, he had gone from the Bronx to Broadway, but much more importantly, he went from the "broad way" to the narrow path which leads to eternal life!

# 2

# Debilitating Fear

"I would have despaired unless I had believed that I would see the goodness of the LORD in the land of the living. Wait for the LORD; be strong, and let your heart take courage; yes, wait for the LORD."

David

It was the fall of 1982. Shannon was a young girl, eleven years of age who looked and acted more like a fifteen-year-old. She was easy to get to know, the type that makes you feel comfortable right away. *Personable* would be one word that accurately described her. She was full of life and full of love.

Kevin Teachey, the fourteen-year-old son of a pastor, was extremely shy. One might even say fearful. In fact, he was so socially awkward that he had great difficulty interacting with other kids. It seemed as if an immovable wall existed between him and others. Although Kevin was a good looking boy, he became increasingly more isolated and disconnected. To escape from his fear of others, he turned to basketball.

One day, he was shooting basketball and daydreaming about making clutch shots under pressure, when suddenly Shannon appeared. Beaming with enthusiasm, she jumped onto the court and boldly asked this boy she'd just met to show her how to shoot a basketball. Kevin was very much "in his element," so he proceeded to interact with her, not realizing how much fun the two of them were starting to have. The laughter grew louder when Shannon shot the ball completely over the backboard. Their laughter subsided and a simple friendship was born. For Shannon it was bliss; for Kevin, it was his very first connection with *anybody*.

The next day Kevin was approached at school by Shannon's older sister who told him that her younger sister was "in love with him." Trying desperately to contain himself, Kevin nevertheless broke out into a wide grin. He had been freed from his prison of isolation, and he could hardly conceal his excitement. Life was going to be good after all! The next few weeks for Kevin and Shannon were somewhat magical--many fun-filled days together on and off the basketball court.

One particular Saturday evening, Shannon was asked to baby-sit for a neighbor. They agreed that Kevin would come over after the mother had left. The thought of being alone together in an apartment started to excite their young minds. Kevin was nervous. On the other hand, he wanted desperately to kiss his newfound love. One thing led to another for the fumbling teenagers that night, and they carried their new thrill of kissing a little further than they should have.

The next day was Sunday, which meant church. Kevin had always had a misconception about God whom he saw as being merciless, ready to strike him dead for the slightest error. As he sat there in church, his tender heart was convicted about the preceding night's events. Exaggerating it into heavy condemnation, Kevin quickly confessed everything to his father. His dad's sharp response stunned him: "Kevin, I forbid you from ever seeing that girl again. Any girl who would let you touch her is *nasty*."

Those words were communicated so forcefully that they

pierced the very soul of this young teen, almost causing him to stumble backwards. It was as if God Himself had thundered down from heaven. Kevin was devastated. Spending time with his new sweetheart was now off-limits--strictly forbidden.

Two days later, Shannon as bubbly as ever showed up at his house. Kevin refused to see her. The next day, the same scenario was sadly repeated. Kevin would not talk to her. Shannon walked away bewildered and confused. Kevin just cried and found another court, far away from Shannon's home, to shoot basketball alone. His spirit was wounded.

A few months later, Kevin was out in his front yard when Shannon approached him cautiously. She was definitely different. Her demeanor was passive. All of her youthful joy was gone. She seemed timid, almost broken. Her only question to Kevin was "What happened?" Uncomfortable and scared to be seen with her, he tried to dismiss the question by saying he had just gotten busy. Shannon knew better and politely asked again. Kevin, unable to make eye contact, struggled for words. Staring down at the ground and pushing the straw on the newly-planted lawn back and forth with his foot, he just shook his head. This was the girl he loved. His eyes began to fill with tears. The awkward moment lingered. Finally, he blurted out, "My father told me that I can't see you anymore!" She stared at him in disbelief. "Why?" she asked, her voice suddenly gaining strength. "Because we went too far that night!" She was completely dumbfounded and offended! Their eyes met briefly, and he could see the tears forming in the corners of her eyes. There was silence. Tears started to flow down her beautiful face. Kevin glanced at her and quickly looked away. She waited. She waited for Kevin to say *something*. Nothing was said. She ran off, sobbing aloud. He forced himself to stand there. To love a girl would be sinful in his eyes. Shannon was nasty.

Kevin immediately went back into his shell. The remainder of his teenage years were very painful. The fear of rejection was overwhelming. During high school he would eat his lunch alone, on the back steps of the gymnasium. One day some other kids invited him to come with them to lunch. He got his nerve up to accept, but the experience proved to be too terrifying. He froze, locked-up right in the middle of the conversation. Claiming to be sick, he ran out of the Burger King. He never allowed himself to get in that kind of situation again.

Years later, he did attempt to have a real relationship with a girl in college who had expressed an interest in him. He was so needy, however, that his erratic behavior simply drove her away. This only served to deepen his conviction that nobody would ever want him once they got to know him. He found himself turning to the world of sexual fantasy where a man could escape and have every dream come true. A place where he would never get hurt.

Upon completing college, Kevin managed to get a job for a finance corporation. Within his first year, he received a prestigious award for his hard work, provoking the business department chairman of his alma mater to invite him to give occasional talks to the freshman students. But the honeymoon of his career in the financial world was coming to an end. He found himself returning to the dark world of pornography more and more. The nastier, the better. In a matter of months, he actually craved it. In fact, he loved it with all his heart. He enjoyed the deception. This sin continued and, over time, took him to a place where he could no longer muster up a sincere smile. He called it his "soul sickness." He felt dead inside.

Now, in his mid-twenties, less than four years after receiving all the accolades of a rising star, he was fired from his job. His life began to unravel once again. His early successes on the job had bolstered his fragile confidence, but now it all fell apart again. In desperation, he called help-lines. He talked to his pastor. He knew he was sinking deeper, but nothing seemed to help him get out of the quicksand. A deep-seated anger began to take control inside. He began cursing, even cursing the name of God, under his breath. In his heart, he despised Jesus. In fact, he hated Him. He was bitter about his life and felt that God had been very unfair to him. However, on Sunday mornings, he would dash to church, many times after having been out drinking and partying the night before.

For three years, he was in psychological counseling weekly. Two years were spent in Alcoholic Anonymous, working the twelve-steps. He also attended Sexaholic Anonymous meetings. He even tried to slow down his thoughts by taking flute lessons. In September of 1996, at the age of twenty-eight, Kevin was beat. Sin had control. He decided to go into a Christian treatment center. Equipped with five weeks of intense positive reinforcement and a nice anti-depressant, he was ready to face the world again after treatment. He lasted only one month, became suicidal, and was rushed back to the treatment center. Embarrassed, he quickly attempted to end his life. An attendant came into the bedroom, just in time, as the cord tightened around his throat.

Two weeks later, he was transferred to the most well-known sexual addiction treatment center in the country. Two additional medications, a thought-organizer, and a mood-stabilizer were pre-scribed to him. He spent an entire month in that secular facility, dutifully completing every exercise given to him. One day, while extremely suicidal, he escaped from the hospital. The staff spent hours looking for him, mostly at the top of tall buildings he might consider jumping from. To their great relief, he returned to the facility. Crying uncontrollably as the staff surrounded him, he made the decision to continue with life. He had just one request. The staff, trying desperately to calm him down, honored his request. A staff counselor escorted him out to the basketball court where Kevin shot basket after basket after basket. His family showed up the next week for a visit. They found him improving gradually, but holding onto a teddy bear the staff had given him for a sense of security. Their twenty-eight year old son had become a shell of a man.

Before long, his insurance ran out and the hospital began looking for somewhere to send him. Not wanting to transfer him to a mental hospital, they were anxious to find anywhere he could go. Someone suggested a Christian rehabilitation center for sexual addicts in Kentucky. Kevin describes his experiences there:

> I arrived at Pure Life Ministries in November of 1996. My first day there the students were taken to a church service. It was too much for me and I ran away, just as I had done at the hospital. The staff was very understanding and supportive when I came back. Jeff Colon had been assigned as my counselor and could see the terror in my eyes. He saw my hopeless-ness and began to work with me intensely. He prayed with me and fought for me when I was discouraged. He taught me how to humble myself.

Pure Life was different, much different, than the other methods I had tried. Within the confines of the live-in program, I was confronted with my sin continuously. The need for "feel better" medication was replaced with a steady diet of prayer and Bible reading. It was incredible how quickly I responded inside. As I began to grow stronger emotionally, I became judgmental of those in leadership. The very people who God was using to save my life now became the targets of my critical spirit. Jeff, a street-wise New Yorker, would have none of that! I was immediately confronted about my attitude. It was the first time that someone didn't baby me. I could handle the strong rebukes Jeff would occasionally give me because I knew he loved me. In fact, I came to realize that the correction I received *was love.*

Gradually, I came into a Reality that was greater than my sin. At Pure Life, Jesus stood tall, positioned squarely in front of me. The blame-shifting was over; it was just Jesus and me. I accepted His mercy and truth.

In 1997, Kevin graduated from the live-in program a changed man. Sin had lost its power over him. Although there was still some evidence of the debilitating fear occasionally, it had definitely lost its hold on his life. Kevin was anxious to get back into the "real world." He landed a job in a mortgage company, which he maintained for almost two years. As he grew disillusioned with the corporate world (all part of God's plan), a dream he had once entertained to attend graduate school began to resurface. He moved to Illinois to begin classes at Wheaton College. Part of this dream, of course, was to find a Christian version of Shannon in college. The wound from the Shannon experience would only be healed by another woman, so he thought. But all of this was Kevin's plan. Although he remained in victory, things were not going well for him. Kevin abandoned his plan to take graduate classes when he sensed the Lord prodding him to give it all up. Kevin, "out on a limb" now, prayed for direction with his mother. In the meantime, another ministry training course was about to begin at Pure Life Ministries and Kevin heard about it. Something jumped inside him. After a two year absence, Kevin returned to Pure Life as a minister trainee.

The next five months were a time of pressing into God in a way he had never experienced before. But just two weeks before he was to graduate, a small incident occurred which sent Kevin reeling inside. Another trainee was selected for a staff position. Although it had nothing to do with him, he became overwhelmed with those old feelings of rejection. Too embarrassed to admit the rejection he felt, he tried to mask it by exaggerating his financial needs and insisting that he needed to go back to secular employment.

He was offered a position paying fairly good money, but it was in Cincinnati. Knowing that the staff at Pure Life would be very concerned about his vulnerability in a big city by himself, he lied about it. Nevertheless, God knew what Kevin was struggling with. As he drove to work on the first day of his new job, his car broke down. Now he wasn't sure what to do. He wanted to confess the whole thing and get right with God, but he still struggled with a lack of trust. He called the ministry office so that someone could come and pick him up. As he was waiting, a couple of very "loose" girls came into the fast food restaurant he was sitting in and began flirting with him. The enemy knew just when to send them. At this point he was really being pulled away from God. He went so far as kissing one of them, but nothing else happened.

He was digging himself in deeper. Unsure about what to do, he called his father for advice. He explained to him that if he told the leadership what he had done, he probably would not be allowed to graduate. "Don't tell them. Just graduate, get out of there and get on with your life," was his father's advice. Those words registered deep within him, just as they had that Sunday afternoon years before. He hung up the telephone. One of the students from the ministry showed up, and for the next forty minutes, "the decision" that would determine the course of his life was decided. This was his great "fork-in-the-road." This was it! His father's admonition was ringing in his ears. His life was in the balance. Whose word should he believe? Whose voice should he obey? "Is God really good? Do Steve and Jeff really love me? Forget about them, does God love me?" All these questions flooded his troubled mind.

He started to remember all the times when he should have died. He thought about his own stubborn will. Tears streaming down his face, a life of pain and rejection descending upon him, and the weight of shame bearing down hard upon his weakened soul, he cried out to his Heavenly Father with all his heart, "it's now or never!" Suddenly a clear thought came into his mind: "If I lose my ability to be honest, I've lost everything." That was all he needed. As soon as they arrived at the facility, he went to Jeff Colon and confessed everything.

Over the next several months, Kevin remained at the ministry, holding down an outside job. He reestablished his walk with God and continued to mature and grow in stability. Meanwhile, Pure Life was busting at the seams with men and needed another counselor. Kevin was approached about the position. There was still one enormous idol in his life: a deeply buried belief that it would require a wife to meet his needs; Jesus was not enough. Being a staff member at Pure Life requires the person to lay *everything* on the altar. How would Kevin respond when told he would have to give up on the idea of *finding a wife*? If it was going to happen, it would have to be completely arranged by God. The Lord helped him to lay this idol down.

I accepted the position at Pure Life Ministries. As part of the job, I am required to attend morning staff meetings and to eat with the staff at dinner each weeknight. I only play basketball now for recreational purposes and no longer as a means of escape. The love I have been searching for, I have found in Jesus, the best friend I've ever had. Whether I ever marry or not, is in His hands. I am preoccupied these days testifying about how trustworthy my Heavenly Father is.

The various wounds I received during my early days have been healed, but I have come to realize that He allowed those wounds so that I would become a seeker of God. I have come to realize that He is also the One who "heals the brokenhearted, and binds up their wounds."

An interesting epilogue to this story is that God allowed Kevin to run into Shannon in 1998. Happily married with four daughters, she was the picture of a perfect American wife--<u>without</u> God. Had Kevin maintained their relationship, they would have, no doubt, become childhood sweethearts. Shannon would have helped him through all the painful days of early manhood. In fact, perhaps having a girlfriend or wife like her would have spared him the suffering and sense of rejection he experienced. Had things unfolded along those lines, Kevin would have grown strong in the love of his wife, instead of being forced to cry out to God for help. He would not have needed the intervention of the Almighty. And, secure in their love for each other, he could have very well become the perfect American husband--<u>without</u> God.

# 3

# The High-minded Star

"Pride goes before destruction, a haughty spirit before a fall." (NIV)

Solomon

Just about every young boy grows up wanting to be a sports star. In backyards all across the nation, kids entertain big dreams about being a star. The scenario runs the same for most: The game is nearing a dramatic end, the crowd is screaming, the pressure is on, and everything depends on the outcome of one individual who usually has extraordinary abilities. Perhaps he is the quarterback. It's the fourth quarter, the clock is ticking, his team down by six points. He takes the snap, the massive defensive end bolts through the line, he side-steps the brute and launches the ball thirty yards downfield. The receiver grabs it in stride and cruises in for the winning touchdown! Or it's the ninth inning, the bases loaded, three runs behind. Down to the last out, the boy sees himself step to the plate. Two screaming fastballs find the mark. Then comes the curveball he's been waiting for. He hits it so hard he can feel a shiver go through his body. The ball sails into the upper deck: a grand slam! For some kids, these dreams turn into reality.

Eddie Smith* was one of those rare boys who was gifted with tremendous talent. It seems that everything he did turned to success. Pushed to excel by parents, coaches and teammates, the innocent childhood dream eventually became an obsession to be-the-best, no matter what. "Just win, baby," became the rallying cry. As he won games and thrilled crowds, a horrible little embryo of pride began to be formed deep within his heart.

As he grew older, the games became bigger, the competition more fierce. Through it all he was being trained to believe in himself, to see himself winning even when all the odds were stacked against him. His performance in high school games gave way to college games. As the stage became bigger; so did his ego. Instead of being the hero of a few hundred, Eddie became the hero of a few thousand. Word of his talent began to spread. One day, someone whispered before a game that a professional scout was in the stands to watch him.

This was the upbringing of Eddie Smith, a young, Christian man who now had the world at his feet. Drafted by a major sports franchise, he quickly became a nationally known star. For awhile, the success was exactly what he had always dreamed of. Fat contracts loaded with financial bonuses, playing in only the biggest cities, staying in the nicest hotels, signing autographs, and so on. All these things kept Eddie's head in the clouds. He had finally arrived. He was "the man."

Not only did Eddie receive the adulation of the sports world but, as a Christian athlete, he was always in demand as a church speaker, a guest on radio and television, and a board member of the most prestigious ministries. Christians love to idolize those who are a success in the world, and Eddie was no exception. In their rush to use him for their own purposes, these men in Christian leadership failed to see that they were actually ruining this young man's life. Instead of discipling him, and encouraging a life of humility and godliness, they thrust him into positions of leadership he should not have held. The Church, the very place this young man should have been able to learn about the narrow path of Christianity, exploited him out of their own selfish ambition.

Eddie was enjoying the heighth of success that this world has to offer. His accomplishments on the field enabled him to achieve more than he had ever dared to envision. But what does a man do when he has achieved "his dream." Some maintain an even keel, do the job, and enjoy the benefits that come with it. Others are blindsided by arriving at the top of the mountain only to discover that nothing fulfilling is there. They begin to frantically search for something that will recreate the "high" they had enjoyed during their meteoric rise to the top. Eddie was such a person.

After several years in the "pros," he was badly injured on the field. Searing pain became his daily companion. He began to search for relief from the unceasing physical distress he was forced to live with. Before long, he found, not just temporary relief from the physical suffering, but also a new thrill to fill the void in his life: crack cocaine. Little by little he lost control. Within a year he was terribly addicted. As this ravishing habit gained control over him, he gradually gave over to an even deeper habit: sexual sin. The two together posed a most formidable foe to his soul.

He continued playing ball, but his problems caused him to begin reaching out for help. He tried going to psychologists and attended various twelve-step groups. He went to clinics and rehabilitation facilities. He had long since given up on finding hope from ministers. At any rate, things only got worse. To further complicate matters, his injury diminished his skills; his career was falling apart.

As time went on, his behavior became increasingly bizarre. Those around him did not know if he was just becoming more eccentric or if something else was at the root of his actions. One night, he got arrested and the word got out that he had a drug problem. His team released him. Now there was nothing to hinder his plunge downward. He was in deep trouble.

One day, Steve Gallagher received a call from an evangelist friend. "Steve, I have someone I want to send out to your live-in program. His name is Eddie Smith. Ever heard of him?"

Having been a sports fan since youth, he knew the name well. "Yeah, I know who he is. What's the problem?"

"He's a mess, Steve. He's all wigged out on crack, but his real problem is sex." He went on to describe some of the things the ballplayer had been into.

"Do you think he has a hunger for the Lord?" Steve asked. "Problems can be overcome; a lack of desire to know God cannot."

"That's the thing, Steve. When he's straight, he really seems to love the Lord. But he just can't seem to keep it together. He's been to half a dozen rehab places, and he does fine for a while, but as soon as he gets out, he's right back to the same stuff. The drugs are making him crazy."

When Steve called Eddie the next day, he seemed like a little kid, scared and broken. His heart went out to him as they talked. Gallagher tried to sound tough with him, letting him know that he would not be given special privileges at Pure Life. Eddie was so full of fear though, that Steve found himself encouraging him. "Why don't you get on a plane, Eddie," Steve told him. "If you really want the Lord, you will find Him here in a very special way."

Kathy Gallagher was not so optimistic about the whole thing. "I was very concerned that some of the men in the program would be star-struck and lose track of why they were there, but Steve was unwilling to turn him away," Kathy recalls. "His argument was that Eddie was as valuable to God as the other men, and he deserved a chance, too."

He arrived about a week later. He looked terrible. It was easy to see he had lost a lot of weight from his playing days. He had been living in a closet of a friend's apartment with a loaded gun close at hand, constantly high on crack.

Totally at the end of himself and almost insane by this time, Eddie responded immediately to the message of God's mercy which is stressed at Pure Life. It began to touch his life in a wonderful way. The Lord's presence was changing him and healing his mind, starting the process of restoring what the drugs and the sex had destroyed. Spending time in the Word of God everyday literally brought sanity to his fearful, tormented mind.

Everything seemed so promising in those early days, but, like so many before and after him, Eddie was coming to his fork in the road. Eddie's greatest problem was not greed, nor worldliness, nor even his obsession with sex. His great, besetting sin was the inordinate amount of pride that had been fostered and nurtured by years of stardom. Even in his playing days, if he did not get the attention he thought he should have, or worse, if someone crossed his will, he would throw a fit. He was known for his hot temper. Even after coming to the place where he was living in a closet with a loaded gun, he remained essentially unbroken. As he began coming back into "sanity," his pride began to rear its ugly head at Pure Life.

At first, it was just over trivial things. He did not like the rules in the live-in program and would simply disregard those which he thought were unnecessary. There is a 10 P.M. curfew in the live-in facility, but if he wanted to eat a snack or talk to one of the other guys, he would do it. When approached about his noncompliant behavior, he would minimize it or shrug it off. As time went on, he grew more arrogant and rebellious.

He did not mind being at a rehab facility. He had promised his wife that he was going to succeed this time. But underneath that apparent willingness to seek help was a definite unwillingness to be taught, much less corrected. In short, Eddie was an unteachable know-it-all. He held the mistaken belief that because he knew so much *about* Christianity, it meant he was much further along than he actually was. He could never understand the fact that a person only really knows what he is actually living in his daily life. He was accustomed to being treated with the respect a superstar automatically inherits. He had a knowledge of the Bible, but it was merely the head-knowledge of someone who doesn't live in the reality of what the Bible teaches. His Christianity was an outward facade of playing the role of the contemporary evangelical. Nobody had ever really challenged him to live out genuine--unselfish--Christianity. In great delusion, he saw himself on a level of spirituality that he was nowhere near. Much of this was directly attributable to those ministers who had exalted him for their own purposes in the past.

His counselor tried to reason with him, explaining to him the importance of obedience in the little things. Eddie would listen, but nothing ever changed. He became increasingly more arrogant and defiant. In a "last ditch" attempt to bring him into reality, his counselor decided to have a "light session" with him in the Tuesday night men's accountability meeting. With Eddie sitting there center stage, each man in the program was asked to share their perspective on the ballplayer's walk with God. Every single man said that he was extremely prideful.

Eddie did not like this very much, but he remained silent. The staff continued their fervent praying for him, hoping that this would be the thing which would turn him around. It was obvious he had come to the fork in the road, but it wasn't clear which way he was turning inside. Although there would be those times when he seemed to soften his heart to the Lord, it was always clear that the underlying attitude was that if he was going to be a Christian it would be on his own terms. The situation continued to deteriorate as he became more difficult to deal with.

It soon became obvious that he had hardened his heart toward the Lord. Knowing what a terrible influence he was having on the other guys there, Steve Gallagher knew he should evict him from the program. In fact, he felt the Lord pressuring him to make him leave. Not totally sure he was hearing from God, and still hoping he would repent, Gallagher hesitated. Eddie had been in the live-in program for five and a half months and was due to graduate in two weeks. He was desperately trying to win his wife back and had promised her that he would not fail this time. But Steve knew he could not graduate a man who was so hard-hearted and unbroken. Finally, he was brought into Steve's office, and humbly told that there was nothing more that could be done for him at Pure Life; he would have to leave.

This shocked him. He was not accustomed to people crossing his will like that. He exploded in a rage, saying, "Oh, you're just like the rest, Steve! I hear a lot about mercy around here -- but I don't see any!" At this he stormed out and slammed the door so hard that it split the wood on the frame. Then he disappeared for a couple of days. He returned to gather up his belongings and was driven to the airport.

The next eight months were extremely painful to those who reached out to him back home. He continued in and out of rehabilitation facilities, seeking the help which he could never seem to find.

One night, he called a local minister crying and begging for help. A few days later, he wrote a letter to his wife expressing his determination to make a new start in life. He was still holding out hope for his career, that he could some day make a big comeback. He met with her, before readmitting himself to a drug rehabilitation facility he had been in before. She embraced him and said gently, encouragingly, "Go get 'em, honey."

One evening, he announced to the staff that he was leaving the facility to go into town. The staff had no choice but to let him go. He went into a rough part of town and purchased some drugs, washing them down with a six-pack of beer. By 11 P.M., he had returned to his house. He called the rehab center. He told them that he had been using and wanted someone to come and pick him up. He had thrown up by the time they arrived about forty-five minutes later. "I'm weary," he told the man. The staff members brought him back to the center, and he went to bed. The next morning, when he had not appeared for breakfast, a staff member went into his room to check on him and found him dead of a drug overdose.

Many things were said about Eddie after he died, but the truth of the matter was that he had come to a vital fork in the road and willfully turned away from God. It would be nice to think that during that final night perhaps he repented and turned to the Lord. These are things that cannot be known on earth. God alone possesses these secrets.

Eddie's life graphically illustrates how fragile life is, how close eternity looms, how our choices on earth affect our everlasting destiny.

# 4

# A Matter of Surrender

"For whoever wishes to save his life shall lose it; but whoever loses his life for My sake shall find it."

Jesus

Lying under the shadows of the massive 59th Street Bridge in Queens, New York, is a predominantly black housing project called Long Island City. Forty to fifty brick buildings stand in close proximity, separated only by the muddy remnants of what was once a beautiful lawn. Each of these five-story apartment buildings houses ten families, which only intensifies the misery and frustration in such congested living quarters.

Jeff Colon (pronounced cologne), on another crack cocaine binge, was in the run-down apartment of a prostitute he had picked up the night before. After three days of constant drug use and two nights without sleep, he was slipping out of reality. (Crack cocaine has the power to bring about tremendous hallucinogenic paranoia.) He went to the bathroom, leaving the prostitute and two men in the living room getting high. Suddenly his mind snapped, and he became convinced that the three of them were out to get him. He locked the door and refused to come out, no matter what they said. The more they tried to convince him, the more "freaked-out" he became.

Finally, Jeff let them in the seedy bathroom. One of the men, a stocky black man in his forties, was carrying a butcher knife. He waved it menacingly in Jeff's face, telling him to get out of the girl's apartment. Interestingly, although he was in a super-paranoid state of mind from being high for three days, Jeff simply did not care if it all ended then and there. He felt as though he could overpower the older man, but the will to fight was gone. He had no intention of leaving and was prepared to die. This was not an idle threat on this man's part. In his own exasperated condition, the only solution he could see was to kill this young Hispanic. Just as he stepped forward to slash Jeff's throat, the other man stepped in front of him and intervened. Once he got the other black man out of the bathroom, he was able to calm Jeff down and convinced him to leave. Somehow, Jeff was able to drive to his home further out on Long Island where he collapsed into a deep sleep.

When Jeff woke up the next day, the reality of how hard-hearted he had become frightened him. He knew he was far from God and in serious trouble. As Jeff considered his options, his mind wandered all the way back to his childhood. He compared the good times of the past to how messed up everything was now. "How did all this happen?" he kept asking himself. Somehow he knew that life was not suppose to be like this!

Jeff grew up in Long Island, New York, in a middle class home. He was blessed to have a good father who taught him solid values and maintained a strict home. God wasn't at the center of this home, but it was still a good home. He was required to attend a Catholic Church and to make his communion and confirmation. Jeff believed there was a God but had no concept of needing a Savior.

At an early age, he began to be involved in a life of drugs and promiscuity just to escape the everyday stresses of life. What began as nothing more than recreational drug use soon developed into a serious habit. Of course, it was inevitable that crime and violence would come with such a lifestyle. Secretly, he began to develop a sexual addiction as well. There were times when he would spend entire nights in hotel rooms smoking crack and watching pornography. This quickly led to an increasing involvement with prostitutes. His father, who was an honorable man, could hardly tolerate seeing his son throw his life away with such waste and nonsense.

When he was 19 years old, God intervened in his life through his oldest sister who was a born-again Christian. One morning, after spending a night in jail for drunk driving and for assaulting two police officers, the reality that his life was going nowhere overwhelmed him. He could see no reason to go on with life. But his sister came and got him out of jail and began sharing the Lord with him on the way home. He began to weep and knew he needed something, so he agreed to go to her church that night. Even though he prayed the sinner's prayer, he continued to struggle with drugs and pornography. The next several years were marked by an up-and-down double life of drugs and sex and Christianity.

In 1991, he married a Christian girl named Rose. Things seemed to be coming together finally. He had gotten a good job as an elevator mechanic, and he and Rose began attending church together. However, Jeff was miserable inside and began disappearing for days at a time to pursue drugs and prostitutes. Finally, with pressure from his family and friends, Jeff admitted himself into Teen Challenge, an Assembly of God drug rehabilitation facility located in Long Island.

Jeff was a good student. He did all his homework, was obedient to his counselors, and remained for the duration of the program. But God wanted more than an outward surrender--He was after Jeff's heart. He successfully completed the program, but what needed to take place inwardly did not happen. Soon after completing the program, he fell back into drugs and sexual sin.

In His mercy, God intervened again; this time it was through the Timothy House, a drug program run by Times Square Church in Manhattan. He spent three months there and again outwardly submitted to what he felt God required of him. Yet, he still held on to his life and what he felt he needed to do with it. Going against the counsel of his wife and spiritual authority, he returned to his job in Manhattan as an elevator engineer. He was simply unwilling to give up the money and worldly success he thought he needed to have. It just did not make sense to him. (Solomon rightly said in Proverbs, "There is a way which seems right to a man, but its end is the way of death.") Jeff was just using his natural, reasoning mind.

He managed to cope with the constant temptations of New York City for about eight months, until his strength and determination finally gave out. Once again, he vanished, leaving Rose sick with worry as he disappeared on another two-day binge. When he came back home, his pastor and wife confronted him. Rose was at the end of her rope. "You can't come home, Jeff. I've had it!"

Jeff's pastor, Jimmy Jack, suggested an alternative to going back into Teen Challenge. "Jeff, you can't come back to church anymore. You're a mess. What I suggest is for you to go to Pure Life Ministries in Kentucky. They deal with sexual sin and I think they can help you."

He was very angry about this ultimatum. He had become so hardened that he was ready to forget God and his whole Christian experience. And yet, as frustrated as he was, he was unwilling to completely turn his back on the Lord. Before the evening was over, he was on a bus to Kentucky.

Upon arrival in Kentucky, Jeff didn't know what to expect at this obscure farm, and one of the first conversations he had [with another student] only increased his anxiety. The student mentioned to Jeff that few men return to their former lives after completing the program. He could not imagine living anywhere but New York. It was the only life he had ever known. A fear gripped his heart that what he said might actually happen to him. He tried to laugh off that statement, but deep in his heart he sensed that those words were prophetic. As they pulled onto the property, Jeff felt very much out of his comfort zone. He quickly made a decision to give God only six months (the length of his Pure Life commitment) to work in his life, or else! Or else, it would be back to the old, wild lifestyle in New York, with no wife and with no God. This was it; one last shot at Christianity.

It did not take long for Jeff to realize that life at Pure Life was much different than anything he had ever experienced before. He could feel God's presence in a very real way. The importance of the outward life, the way he acted in front of others, was de-emphasized and more focus was given to the daily inward life. God began showing Jeff that He was looking for a true change in his heart. He was not going to be able to simply conform to the rules of the program as he had in the past. The Lord began showing Jeff what a hypocrite he had been, challenging him to begin living what he claimed to believe. This self-confident engineer was being broken, one day at a time, one issue at a time.

In the "dog-eat-dog" world of New York street life, Jeff had learned how to hate his enemies with all his heart. This deeply entrenched attitude was tested early in the program when he was forced to get along with a difficult roommate. Over time, Jeff began to detest him to the point that he couldn't even look at him. Nevertheless, wanting to obey God, he kept his feelings to himself. He did his best to tolerate the man. But the Lord hadn't commanded him to tolerate his enemy; he was expected to love him. God began revealing how unmerciful he was in his heart and began to urge him to pray for that man.

Jeff was at a real crossroad. It was clear to him that to go on with Jesus meant to love those around him--"all" those around him. Every attempt at rationalization, every effort to sidestep this central issue, every attempt to point the finger, left Jeff feeling hopelessly defeated. Criticizing the brother only caused Jeff to see his own glaring pride and high-mindedness. Jeff was in his own self-imposed prison and he knew it. He had to cry out to God for help, OR ELSE it was all over. Jeff did the one thing his counselor had told him to do: he humbled himself and prayed earnestly for that brother.

At first, praying for the other man seemed ineffective and false. Jeff's words would just fall straight to the ground without any life in them at all. Day after day, he would ask God to bless this brother, meeting his needs with life-fulfilling mercies. He didn't feel anything, but he was determined that he was going to do what he was taught at Pure Life. If it didn't work here, he was going to walk away from God and never come back.

One day while he was on "the prayer trail," Jeff saw his "enemy" through God's eyes. He began to break and weep in a true compassion for the man's soul. He knew what he was feeling was not from his own heart; it was God's heart breaking over the man's needs. Jeff was experiencing what the Lord goes through over hurting people everywhere, all the time.

But this was not all that was happening inside him. Thoughts of the past flooded Jeff's mind. He remembered the guy waving the knife at him in that prostitute's apartment. He remembered the tears of his loving wife, pleading with him to get help and surrender his life to Jesus. He remembered his pastor standing firm against his flesh and ordering him to go to Pure Life Ministries. All these memories came crashing down upon him and they all pointed to one word: MERCY! Suddenly, all the mercy God had lavished upon him became very real. He fell in a heap before Him, overwhelmed with the magnitude of God's love for people; overwhelmed with how little love he had shown to others. He was broken like he had never been broken before. At that moment, he knew he could love this man, in fact, he knew he could love anybody. It was God's love flowing through his being!

This was a huge breakthrough in Jeff's life, but his real fork in the road was still ahead of him. Several months into the program, God had really begun to do a work in his heart. He was revealing His will to Jeff and made it clear to him that He expected him to live out *everything* he had been taught.

One evening, his counselor told him that he might never return to New York. It was almost exactly what that other student had said when he first arrived at Pure Life. His whole being shook inside when he heard those words. The fear was so real that he literally felt cold. Jeff had always been an obsessive controller. The Lord was dealing with him about letting go of his own plans, letting go of the reins of his life. He shares what he experienced:

> No matter how hard I tried to avoid or evade it, God kept pressing me about this issue in meetings, homework, counseling, and things I read in my Bible. God was tugging at my heart. I had been in the program for about five months when the Lord spoke very clearly to my inner man one day when I was out on the ridge praying. "You are not going back to your old life. I want you to leave all behind and serve Me."

Oh, how I wrestled that day with God! I felt like my whole insides were being torn to pieces. I knew God was speaking to me and I knew if I didn't yield to God's will, my life would be miserable and I would be in trouble.

I wanted to live this consecrated life, but I wanted to do it in New York, not Kentucky. I wanted it to fit into my own life. But the Lord made it very clear to me that day that there were two roads before me. One was narrow and had no room for my own plans or what was comfortable for me. The other was broad and had plenty of room for what I wanted to do, my life in New York, my career, my possessions and even a little place for Jesus.

I finally gave in to God and chose the narrow way. The minute I made the choice, all the pressure, anxiety, and turmoil left and a peace that surpasses all understanding came upon me. I immediately ran up and called my wife. Victory, at last!

Unbeknownst to him, God was laying the same thing on his wife's heart back in New York. Jeff called Rose and told her to put everything up for sale--they were moving to Kentucky. They spent the next six months seeking God, learning what it means to minister His love to others, being taught how to counsel biblically. Within two years of graduating the intern program and coming on staff, Jeff was appointed as the director of the live-in program.

When one of his counselees struggles with making that full surrender, Jeff's mind immediately goes back in time to his great battle with God out on the "prayer trail." He sympathizes with the man's struggle, and then shares his own story: "I remember what a struggle I had with surrender when I came to Pure Life....."

Jeff and Rose are both sterling examples of what it means to live under the control of the Holy Spirit. They have no home of their own, no savings account, few worldly possessions. But what they do have is a deep, abiding love for Jesus that has affected many people's lives across the nation. Jeff Colon's surrender has translated into a deeply fulfilling and fruitful life.

# 5

# Overwhelming Temptation

"Blessed is a man who perseveres under trial; for once he has been approved, he will receive the crown of life, which the Lord has promised to those who love Him."

James

In 1996, after three long, excruciating years in the classroom setting, the day every medical student looks forward to had finally arrived for one young aspiring doctor: Part I of the National Board Examination. At last, it was time to apply what he had been taught and had spent countless hours studying for. Brad Furges was completing his third year of medical school, but on May 30th, he was placed on suspension for being late to take a weekly drug test. Now, everything Brad had worked for was swinging in the balance--it was a nightmare he could hardly believe. After several weeks of counseling, he reappeared before the Dean of Students in August of that year, hoping to be readmitted to school. However, much to his dismay, the dean suggested that he explore further his personal issues surrounding his history of non-compliance and promised to reconsider his re-admission in November. That meant the leaves would have to change colors before Brad would even know if he still had a medical career to look forward to. Unable to cope with all this and unwilling to accept responsibility for his actions, Brad lost all hope of ever becoming a doctor and became totally isolated from his friends, family, and even God. He sought a way out of this harsh reality. Unfortunately, to escape the pain he was now facing, he turned to the same deadly combination of sex and drugs that had brought about his medical school failure.

Drug abuse was a secondary problem in Brad's life. It came about in large part because of his painful struggle with homosexuality. It all began as a young boy when he and one of his cousins experimented with homosexuality. This continued off and on over the next several years until 1983 when Brad was in the ninth grade. It was then that his cousin, through malice or jealousy, spread it around school that Brad had made a "pass" at him, rather than admit that both of them consented to their secret activities. The news spread quickly. All of Brad's closest friends heard the rumor. He was consumed with fear because in high school, kids tend to be quite vicious and quick to label anyone with wayward tendencies as an outcast--a contagious, untouchable, undesirable pervert... Although he vehemently denied such an accusation, in his mind this was enough to satisfy anyone's suspicion that he was indeed gay--after all, there *was* an element of truth to the matter. Needless to say, this one incident devastated him and left him with a deep sense that he did not fit in with anyone--no one knew the real Brad. Life to him seemed only to be filled with gloom and doom. He felt paralyzed--emotionally disturbed... abnormal... hopeless... ashamed... rejected. He describes what he went through:

> Guilt and shame overwhelmed me. I became
> very depressed. Just getting up in the morning was a
> chore--another miserable day that I had to walk around
> with an imaginary badge which read "Yes, I'm gay. It's

true!"

Growing up, I had often been teased and called "faggot" or "sissy" because I was very studious and did not play sports and run the streets like the rest of the fellas' my age. Usually, I was unmoved by such name-calling--I had a "sticks-and-stones-may-break-my-bones-but-words-will-never-hurt-me mentality. However, at this traumatic point in my life, I now came to the painful realization that I was guilty of doing what they had accused me of, or what they thought about me all along! I did not think that there was another person on God's "green earth" going through what I was experiencing; I saw absolutely no hope.

However, one particular night I went to my room with tear-filled eyes and I opened my little New Testament Bible and read John 8:32: "And ye shall know the truth and the truth shall make you free." That should have been Good News to me, but because I did not have any comprehension or understanding of such a precious promise, I was even more condemned than ever... I had lied to everyone... I would never be free... No one could ever know the truth. I told my mom during this period that "I will never have a normal life."

Unable to come to terms with what I considered an unpardonable sin, my life became consumed with anything having to do with sex or sexuality. I immediately began to read literature (books, magazines, newspaper articles, etc.) to research any issue dealing with homosexuality or bi-sexuality. I read the Kinsey studies on male sexuality to try to discover if I fit the criteria of being gay or bi-sexual. So from junior high until college (1984-1987) I was on what I thought was a search to discover "Brad." Needless to say, I did not find him!

At the same time all of this was going on, Brad was becoming increasingly addicted to sexual activity as his knowledge and awareness of sexual trends and behavior throughout history was broadened. In the back of his mind, he hoped that maybe there were others out there somewhere who shared the same struggles as he did. Eventually, he became more aware of his own sex drive and began to masturbate compulsively. He was somewhat attracted to girls but was much more intrigued with men. He started taking special notice in men's physique, studying their macho behavior and comparing himself with them. In Brad's eyes, he never measured up nor could he ever. It was obvious to him that the good-looking, muscular athletic types won the hearts of most of the girls. He envied the popularity of such "pretty boys." Nevertheless, he longed for their acceptance. Although he tried to take an interest in girls, his attraction for and obsession with men began to increase. However, the day finally came for him to leave home, his friends, and his past behind... opportunities to meet new people, to go new places, to explore life, and to have new experiences--college. This was Brad's D-day! Freedom at last!

But for Brad, the freedom he now felt only brought about a deep bondage to homosexual sin and eventually, crack cocaine. His entire four years of college became a blur of sex, partying, and late-night study sessions.

In November 1991 he got wonderfully saved. In his newfound faith, he broke away from his old relationships and became very zealous for the Lord. He was thrilled to be delivered from drugs and serving the Lord, but he still had that uncontrollable urge and desire for men. Because the temptations became overwhelming, he began to question his salvation. After only four months as a Christian, he relapsed into perversion and drug use. Over the next three years, as he continued on in his academic pursuits, he continually fell back into drugs and sex with brief, intermittent periods of "sobriety."

By 1995, he had totally given over to the gay lifestyle. He was convinced that "coming out of the closet" would help him in his recovery from drug addiction, but he soon discovered that it only made things worse. Things continued to unravel in Brad's life until the following year when he was dismissed from medical school. Now there was nothing to hinder him from plunging deeper and deeper into sin. All the props had been removed from his life.

By the fall of 1996, Brad was coming to an end of his rope. He knew he needed to do something. It was then that he became involved with Evangel Fellowship Church in Greensboro, North Carolina. Elder Cliff Lovick, the director of a Christian drug rehabilitation home that was affiliated with the church, took a real interest in Brad's life.

In May, 1998, Brad went on a five day crack binge. His family was sick with concern. In an attempt to reach out for help, he called a friend named Ricky from church. They met across the street from a local adult bookstore. Ricky convinced him to go see Elder Lovick that night. Exhausted, with no fight left in him, he agreed. It was past midnight when Brad pulled into the driveway. To his surprise, the godly old man came running out to welcome him back. Brad felt humiliated. He was "tore up from the floor up" ...and smelled like an outhouse.

Brad spent the next eight months going through the program at the Malachi House. The Lord used this time to bring Brad's life under control and get him headed in the right direction. In the meantime, a former student who had been sent to Pure Life Ministries to deal with sexual sin shared about the deep work God had done in his life there. Knowing Brad's inner struggles, Elder Lovick suggested he too go through the program at Pure Life. He arrived in March, 1999. He shares some of his first impressions:

> Because I only went there to deal with "*my* issues" (which centered only around my struggles with homosexuality), humbling myself to others or even being merciful to an undeserving individual were concepts foreign to me and of no great interest to me. However, as I began to read *Sexual Idolatry*, I was exposed. I got my first glimpse of how corrupt I was and how ignorant I was of the true character and nature of God despite the fact that I professed in my testimony which I sent in that "I love God." Page by page and chapter after chapter, I saw that I was guilty as charged -- a sinner without excuse. Who was I to blame now? Could it really be true that I was responsible for all the sin and degradation I wallowed in for years? Nevertheless, I found hope... there was a way out that I did

not quite understand yet.

Brad's will was crossed countless times in the months ahead. The Lord was trying to teach him that if he was ever going to escape from the prison of "self" he had lived in for so many years, he would have to learn to love other people and humble himself to them. The more he resisted this, the more miserable he became inside. Getting "in it," having major conflicts with brothers at the home and on his job, characterized the first four months of his life at Pure Life. His critical, judgmental, unmerciful heart was continually exposed. This was not easy and yet, Brad knew that God's hand was in the process in a powerful way. Refusing to give up or lose hope, he continually cried out for help.

Just when it seemed as though he could not take another trial in life, he was forced to deal with his sexual lust. This had not been a real problem during the first few months of the program, but then another young black man showed up who was also out of the gay lifestyle. Brad shares his reflections on how this affected him:

A man named Jake became my first struggle with overwhelming temptation and desire for the forbidden. The "wrestling match" between my flesh and God's Spirit commenced. God mercifully used my struggles with Jake to expose what was buried deep within my heart... a wicked, evil, disobedient, and rebellious nature that utterly refused to be denied access to something that was tantalizing or seemingly gratifying.

Before long, after several unwholesome conversations looking back at the "old days" of sin and insanity, Jake and I knew that we definitely came out of the same cesspool. Rather than being a real blessing to him, I began to entertain thoughts... lustful thoughts. I was overwhelmed with curiosity... "need-to-know spirit." I wanted to know whether or not I could have been able to "book" Jake out in the world. Yes, I was treading dangerous territory, looking back at Sodom... deceived nonetheless. Unbeknownst to me, my idolatrous feelings were slowly leading me back down the path of backsliding. I entered the following statement in my journal on 6/07/99:

> Separate/separation... Lord, help me to obey Your word. Please deliver me from a spirit of lust. Please make me a man of character and a vessel full of Your Holy Spirit so that I will love the way You have commanded me to and to hate what You hate.

### Almost one month later, I wrote on 7/01/99:

> I must mention that I am quite glad that Jake and I have been separated. Things were getting out of hand. We began to lust for each other like we were "children" (homosexual slang referring to other gay men) in the streets. Surely, I will not fall for the same old lies of the Devil again. The word says 'submit yourself therefore to God, resist the Devil and he will flee from you.' I did not exactly do this. Although I have been pretty open with Jeff and George about our struggles with one another, I entertained unwholesome thoughts, I allowed my imagination to run wild, I even sought to get very close to him without having to tell anyone. LIES! I agonized over my feelings and desire for him for over three weeks.

### Still struggling on 7/03/99:

> I am going through a serious test. All I'll say is Jake. The more we are apart the more we are drawn to one another. He is forbidden! I am forbidden! Choices! Life is full of them! Choices! Jesus, help me! Save me from myself! Deliver me, O God! Set me free! Lord, if you don't help me I am liable to give in to temptation. My mood did a major phase shift when Jeff separated Jake and I. "Let us be! Go away! But I want It!" I cried. I ache inside--I simply ache. Lord, help me before I lose it! I know that the only way out is to resist & separate but something inside me is totally against doing these simple but crucial acts of obedience! Help now, Lord!

As much as they toyed with the thought of it, it is amazing that Brad and Jake kept themselves from running away together. Several times, during that period, Jeff Colon was ready to ask them both to leave, but each time, he felt the Lord restrain him. In the meantime, the two of them continued to battle with overwhelming temptation. The staff couldn't see it at the time, but Brad was growing in strength through the whole ordeal. Just when it seemed as though he was going to make it through, he and Jake hugged each other inappropriately. He describes what he went through after this incident:

I was devastated. I felt like I had just smoked crack and was out of money. Totally empty. Full of guilt. Full of fear. All the next day, I repented and asked God to help me out of this once again. What was the problem? We did not actually act out completely. Why the guilt, shame, and fear? My conscience was tearing me up. I could run but where was I to hide. God knew... He saw. My sin was ever before me. I was in such great despair... worldly sorrow nonetheless... because I knew that there was a good chance that I would get thrown out of here this time after being repeatedly warned over the last two months. The ridiculous thought came in my mind to consider moving to Cincinnati with Jake if we did get kicked out. Wait! Wait one minute! No way! I did not come all the way out here to not get what I came here for... to get "my issues" dealt with! What other ministry was out there to confront my sin and offer me hope and a way out of myself... into Jesus Christ. What am I crazy?

The questions that I had to ask myself as the war raged between my spirit man and my flesh: "What about your family? Are you willing to disappoint them once again... to hurt them once more... to have them worried sick because you are somewhere lost, missing in action? After all God has brought you through and done for you, you are going to settle for this madness? This was the first time in my life that I really counted the costs and considered my family. I had never examined the consequences... the "end of the matter" or how my actions would affect the lives of others. I knew I had to go to God to bail me out once more! I felt almost healed over this Jake saga at this point. Enough was enough. Play time was definitely over. I no longer needed a restriction.

Jake pleaded with me that morning not to tell, fearing that because I had gone to staff previously when we struggled that I would reveal our latest encounter. I knew that confession was the only way out. I had previously stood on Proverbs 28:13... He *who covers his sins will not prosper, but whoever confesses and forsakes them will have mercy.* This is the only promise I had to stand on which gave me the strength and courage to bring this thing into the light. I could not have imagined going through the motions and not confessing it to staff. God is a God of Mercy at Pure Life but He is also a God of Exposure too. Sin cannot hide there.

So that evening after work, I told Jake we had to go to Steve Gallagher... "Steve Gallagher? You're crazy!" was his reply. Mr. Gallagher's serious devotion to God terrified us both. Nevertheless, I drug Jake with me to see him. To my utter amazement, he did not rebuke us. He questioned us and seemed to empathize with our struggle. In fact, he said, "I can't imagine what it would be like if I were living in a place surrounded by women." Then, looking me in the eye, he got very strong and told me firmly, "Stay away from Jake. Look at me. You stay away from Jake." I humbly replied, "Yes, sir." It was just what I needed. There were no more episodes, no more struggles after that.

From this point on, Brad and Jake were headed in two different directions. It wasn't long after this incident that Jake was asked to leave. Brad had a real struggle with temptation, but he also had a genuine desire to overcome and grow closer to God. Jake, on the other hand, lacked that sincerity.  He became increasingly more prideful and rebellious.  Like many others before him, he had to go.

With Jake out of the picture, Brad really began to press into the Lord.  When he graduated the live-in program in December, he was invited to enter the Pure Life ministerial training program where his spiritual life wonderfully blossomed.  Had he had a say in the matter, he would have avoided the overwhelming temptation which Jake's appearance presented.  But the Lord knew exactly what he needed and what he could handle.  Bradley made it through the fiery test and came out the other end as silver refined in the crucible.

Now he has a bountiful life in God.. Instead of the gloomy, depressed person he used to be, he is a bubbling fountain of the joy of the Lord.  He has become a vital part of the work which goes on at Pure Life Ministries.

# 6

# Seeing the Beam

"No one who has a haughty look and an arrogant heart will I endure."

The Lord

Almost eight years after the assassination of President John F. Kennedy, the National Cultural Center in Washington, D.C. officially opened and was dedicated to his memory. In a front page story, the New York Times stated, "The capital of this nation finally strode into the cultural age tonight with the spectacular opening of the $70 million (Kennedy Center)... a gigantic marble temple to music, dance, and drama on the Potomac's edge." From the beginning it developed a reputation of hosting only the very finest productions in the performing arts.

It was about ten years after the dazzling opening of this national memorial that a young pianist, named Lance Baker,* got his big break. He was hired as a dance accompanist with a prestigious ballet company. The next seven years were a whirlwind of playing before packed audiences in the most famous theaters, opera houses, and performing arts centers in the world. Several times during this period the ballet company performed on national television as well. There were even occasions when the young pianist was asked to play as a soloist.

However, it was in 1985, that Lance experienced the absolute pinnacle of success. His ballet troupe appeared at the Kennedy Center before President and Mrs. Ronald Reagan. Playing before the Commander-in-Chief and the First Lady was an unforgettable event that few ever experience. The performance was flawless and Lance was ecstatic! It was a breathtaking experience for this young man who had had such a painful childhood.

Lance grew up in a small Midwestern city. He never knew his real father and had to deal with his mother's marriage to another man while he was still a young boy. At the tender age of eleven, tragedy struck when his mother died. Suddenly, he felt very alone. Although his step-father was a decent man, he was a strict disciplinarian--a strong man who showed little affection. Before long, he remarried, which meant yet another major adjustment for Lance. Emotionally, this was too overwhelming for this adolescent to deal with.

However, life seemed much more promising two years later when he had an encounter with the Lord at a church youth rally. Even though he had regularly attended church, Sunday school, youth fellowship, choir practice and Boy Scouts at the formal church he grew up in, this was the first time he ever truly heard the gospel of salvation preached and then followed with an altar call. He describes what happened:

> My heart was electrified, and I practically ran down to the altar when the invitation was given. Unfortunately, even though I tried to pray and read the Bible and continue my activities at my home church, I had no one to disciple me further, so my newfound faith and enthusiasm gradually began to wane. Puberty further complicated things, and I began to mas-

turbate and to experiment sexually with boys from school. Unable to bear the guilt of sexual sin but unable to stop it, I started to avoid God, and by the time I graduated from high school, I had tuned Him out completely.

During my senior year in high school I decided I was "gay," and I lived for the day that I'd graduate and be out on my own. When I finally got my "freedom," I wasted no time before immersing myself in the homosexual lifestyle.

While the other high school boys played sports, Lance turned his attention to learning how to play the piano. Before long, it became obvious to his teachers that he was very gifted. Responding to their encouragement, he threw all his energies into training to become a concert pianist. His newfound homosexual identity went hand-in-hand with his talent, and he soon began to play for dance classes and rehearsals at a local ballet company. He excelled as a dance accompanist, which eventually led to the opportunity with a nationally-known ballet troupe. It was this organization that was responsible for his appearing at the Kennedy Center. After playing for the Reagans, Lance was on top-of-the-world! He had achieved everything he had ever wanted in life--respect in the music industry, extensive tours, and an appearance before "royalty."

As his success increased, his addiction to homosexual sin grew as well. At first, he enjoyed the excitement of new relation-ships. The deeply rooted feelings of childhood rejection were masked and seemed to be replaced with the sense that he was actually *wanted*. However, he would one day realize that--"the peace that the world gives"--is not like that which the Lord offers.

Eventually, he began to grow dissatisfied. His performances grew stale and the applause had become unrewarding. Playing for the president was a distant memory. With an endless array of men, each new encounter simply became yet another meaningless, degrad-ing, and humiliating experience for him. Lance became increasingly morose and difficult to be around. The more miserable he became, the more he sought fulfillment in sexual experiences, spending nearly all his free time "cruising" adult bookstores, parks, and public rest rooms.

Out of desperation, he decided a change was needed. He moved to Reno, Nevada, and landed a job as a poker dealer. Lance's unflappable exterior paid off as a dealer, leaving the best card players around unable to guess what was in his hand. Somehow, he began feeling excited about life again. The neon lights... the fast action and interactions... the flow of cash from one hand to the next... the significant others. This was it! Paradise on earth! A sense of purpose--a sense of fulfillment! So, Lance set out to become a professional poker player. For several months, he saved nearly every dime he earned working for the casino, stockpiling a bankroll which he would some day use to launch his new career. Playing for the casino was acceptable for the time being, but Lance, totally caught up in the "spirit" of this gain-seeking environment, had greater ambitions in mind. He wanted the opportunity to win big money for himself.

One night, the man he was with took some amphetamines. Lance had always avoided drugs but decided he would try them. He began taking uppers to keep him going and to enhance sex, but before long he started using cocaine, "speed" and then, "crack." The crack cocaine became like a ravenous beast. Lance, who had always prided himself on his cool, controlled demeanor, had a severe addiction. He quickly blew threw his savings. Pretty soon his dream ended in misery. Lance hit bottom pretty hard this time and began searching for help. He desperately needed answers.

In drug rehab, he was introduced to twelve-step programs which caused him to surrender to the idea that he was powerless over sex and drugs and needed a "higher power." For several years he had alternating periods of recovery and relapse before he knew for sure that his "Higher Power" was none other than Jesus Christ. However, the way of the cross seemed too difficult and harsh compared to the so-called unconditional love heralded by new-agers. He resisted Christianity until finally, after a horrible relapse, he realized that his way was not effective. He went to church and surrendered his heart to the Lord. A couple days later, he met with the pastor who led him in the sinner's prayer.

Lance's problems weren't over yet. He still had the homo-sexuality issue to contend with. He knew that his promiscuous lifestyle was sinful, but he held onto his belief that two men could somehow have a committed relationship blessed by God. He wrestled with this question for months until he finally just believed what the Bible said was true -- that homosexuality was an abomination to Him. Full of fear and doubting whether he could ever really change, he prayed for God's forgiveness and asked if He could somehow, someway change his sinful lust. The Lord was merciful. The very next night he heard Steve Gallagher on the radio. God had provided help when he was ready to receive it. For the first time, he heard a real message of hope by someone who had once been heavily bound to sexual sin himself but had been set free.

He immediately ordered *Sexual Idolatry,* Steve Gallagher's book which outlines the biblical steps to overcoming sexual addiction. He began trying to put those principles into practice, but he found it tough going. He was too new to Christianity, and the pressures of Reno were so great that he had a lot of difficulty walking in victory for any length of time. He felt the Holy Spirit's pressure to surrender and leave Reno and move to the Pure Life live-in program in Kentucky. He realized there could be no turning back. Lance was not going to Kentucky simply to be cleaned up a bit or to obtain a few self-improvement tips. He had to burn his bridges by selling and giving away almost everything he owned. The hardest part was letting go of his nine-year old cat that he had raised from a kitten. But everything had to go--piano, TV, photos, books, records, stereo, and furniture.

Ironically, that was the easy part. When he got to Kentucky, he soon found out that he still had tons of baggage deep within the crevices of his heart. Years of self-pity had built up, along with deep fears, resentments, arrogance, worldly wisdom and sophistication. As these layers of selfishness began to be peeled away, there were many times he wanted to run back to Reno.

As God was exposing the ugliness of his heart, he began looking at the faults of those around him in an attempt to make himself feel or look better. He began to seek ways to discredit the ministry and its leaders. True enough, it was not hard to find things to criticize. As the leaders of a fledgling ministry, Steve and Kathy Gallagher were stretched too thin in those days: answering telephones, doing the books, responding to mail, doing the manual work on the property during the day, counseling at night, and travelling to various cities to preach in churches on the weekends. This was 1990, and the program was only a few months old. It didn't seem like a legitimate ministry in those early days. At one point, there was even a mass exodus. Almost everybody left. The Gallaghers were crushed by it. Lance wanted to leave, too, but unlike the others, he wouldn't go because he was determined to obey the Lord.

Gradually, God began to do a work in his heart as he accumulated days, weeks, and months of freedom from sexual sin. At the same time, the Lord began to bring in other guys who were committed to enduring, and the program started to come together. Lance was determined to do what was right, but it was very obvious he had numerous other problems to work through.

Most of the time he was a very pleasant person to talk to. However, Lance was also very moody, and his mood swings usually dictated how he treated others. There were times he would sink into a black pit of gloom and despair, where everything appeared hopeless to him. He would become sullen and depressed, seeing only the negative in life and being highly critical of everyone around him.

On top of all this, Lance was very arrogant, but not in the normal loud, obnoxious manner. His haughtiness was more of a quiet smugness of superiority, having a disdain for anyone who was not on his intellectual level. Although he usually concealed such thoughts, there were times that this attitude was quite obvious to those around him.

Lance did begin to slowly change. About four months into the program, he faced a major test when he was offered a job as a pianist. Securely anchored deep within his heart was a great love for this world. Its pull silently and steadily began to exert its force upon Lance's wavering heart. Memories of standing ovations and fine restaurants flooded his mind. He was back swimming in the ocean of self-glory again, when a sudden calm came over his soul. Sanity returned. A decision was made. Lance chose to follow Jesus. It was one of those hurdles that many do not get by. This was his first fork in the road and one can only imagine the heartache he was spared by obeying the voice of God.

When Lance graduated the live-in program, he was invited to come on staff. He had a great determination to know the Bible and learn about the things of God. It was not long before he became the primary counselor for the men. He spent his days studying the principles of biblical counseling and his evenings in the actual practice of it. The early days were rough, but it was not long before God really developed him into a first-class counselor.

However, Lance still harbored selfish attitudes that God would go after in the days to come. For example, problems arose when he started befriending stray cats that came onto the PLM farm. Before long, there were nine cats living there, which were simply nuisances on the property. At first, he stubbornly refused to get rid of the cats, but when he was shown how he was putting them ahead of the good of the men who had to live there, he agreed to send them to the pound. This repentance temporarily relieved the problem, but the issue would rear its ugly head again later.

Months rolled by, men came and went, many of whom experienced tremendous change in their lives. Lance's responsibility increased in the ministry. He deserved it because of the great way God was using him. However, there was a deep-seated arrogance within him that the Lord had yet to expose and deal with.

As time went on, he became increasingly more critical of others. He rose up in pride and saw himself as being spiritually superior to his leaders. He became more and more self-righteous. He was so consumed with the specks in the eyes of others that he became unwilling to see the beam in his own eye. He became stuck spiritually and was no longer growing.

In 1994, he was confronted about his highmindedness. To everyone's surprise, he openly acknowledged his prideful attitude and agreed that he needed to change. Just bringing the issue into the light could have--*should have*--produced a marvelous spiritual breakthrough for Lance. Had a sincere repentance occurred in his heart, the Lord would have helped him to come down a few notches in his own mind. But deep inside his heart he was unwilling to relinquish his exaggerated opinion of himself. He was unwilling to simply be *a regular guy*. He had always felt a need to be special. Unfortunately, this usually came at the expense of those around him.

After the staff confronted Lance about his pride, he became more careful about how he handled himself outwardly, but inside, he remained essentially unbroken. His acknowledgment of the pride was only words, no heartfelt repentance was experienced. It all came to a head one day when Lance became enraged with the Gallaghers over a cat they wanted to take to the pound. He slammed his fist onto their coffee table and stormed out of their house. When that happened, they knew inside that the time had come for him to go. Steve called the members of the Pure Life board; a unanimous decision was made to release him from staff.

With tears in his eyes, Steve told him he would have to leave Pure Life. The look of absolute astonishment on his face that day belied the fact that he considered himself as being indispensable and irreplaceable.

As he packed his bags, an idea came to the staff that perhaps he could be sent to another ministry for a period of restoration. Steve became very excited at the prospect of him coming back to PLM, hopefully, a little more humbled. He called the director of another rehabilitation facility and explained the situation to him, asking him if he were willing to have Lance go through his program as a student. It was clearly conveyed that he would be expected to be restored to Pure Life within six months. He agreed. Lance acknowledged that it was the very thing he needed.

Unable to conceal his emotions, Steve openly cried as he drove Lance to the other ministry. He simply could not believe that it had come to this. Lance sat quietly, almost in a daze. Steve left him there and made the long drive home.

Anxious to find out how he was doing, Steve called the other minister the following week. "He's doing great!" came the reply "I have already made him a counselor here!" Steve was sick inside when he heard those words. This was the worst thing that could have happened to Lance. What he needed was to learn to live in submission to authority, not be thrust right back into leadership himself. "But you promised he would be a student," Steve lamented. "This is going to ruin him!"

The other minister simply replied, "That was before I knew about his walk with God. Nobody is going to tell me what to do with a man in my program." Steve felt hurt, betrayed and broken when he got off the telephone. Lance wasn't simply an employee; he was part of the family.

The PLM staff kept hoping that he would be able to return,

but over the months it became painfully evident it was not going to happen. In the meantime, the other ministry began to flounder. In 1995, the minister in charge of it had left. It quickly fell apart after that. Although Steve talked with Lance, still hoping he would return to Pure Life, it quickly became obvious that he was as prideful as he had ever been. There was not going to be reconciliation.

It was later discovered that Lance had left the ministry to move to another city. In time, he went back into drugs and the homosexual lifestyle. He struggled for a couple of years before he finally, once again, found the freedom he had had at Pure Life. Now Lance is a waiter in a restaurant living from paycheck to paycheck. He occasionally falls but still attends church.

One might wonder what might have come from his life had he allowed God to really humble him! Instead of serving tables, by this time he would be walking in a wonderful depth of God. He has spent years suffering the consequences of his unwillingness to allow the Lord to deal with his pride.

Even worse is the loss that the kingdom of God has suffered from his decisions. In the years since he left Pure Life, hundreds of men could have been impacted by his life. The rest of the story would have been full of life-changing testimonies of men who were led to victory over sin by Lance's ongoing example. Tragically, however, such a breaking never came.

# 7

# God's Work of Restoration

"Brethren, even if a man is caught in any trespass, you who are spiritual, restore such a one in a spirit of gentleness... Bear one another's burdens, and thus fulfill the law of Christ."

The Apostle Paul

Paranoid schizophrenics are liable to do anything at any given moment. The slightest thing can trigger "an episode." Family members are constantly on guard, never knowing what to expect from the tormented loved one. Only someone who has lived with a person disturbed like this can comprehend the anxiety and often fear that permeates such a home.

Phil Shepherd* was a young boy when his mother was diagnosed as a "paranoid schizophrenic." The early years of his life were full of violent strife. His mother would go into one of her "spells" so often that he and his sister learned early on to go through the house collecting knives and scissors to guarantee her safety and their own. On any given day, during any given hour, he did not know what his mother might do next. Because of her ongoing battles, the family was kept at a heightened alert at all times.

It was tough for Phil to see his mother disconnected from reality. It was even more difficult when he saw her committed to institutions or mental hospitals, time-and-time again. This was the woman who brought him into this world. He was a small boy, needing love and affection. His mother was sick, unable to help and unable to nurture him. His father was a brilliant man, but by the time Phil was born, he was emotionally lifeless. Among other occupations he mastered in his life, he was a medical doctor. When Phil was about three years of age, his father was sent to prison, where something dreadful happened to him. He was never the same after that. Phil and his sister were forced to live in foster homes. It was in one of these homes that both he and his sister were raped. Much damage was done, needless to say. This traumatic ordeal almost destroyed their lives.

As he reached his teenage years, like most young people going through puberty, Phil began experimenting sexually. He became consumed with the idea of having a girlfriend, feeling as though he had to have a girlfriend to be accepted by the other guys. Who the girl was or what she looked like was not overly important; he just had to be going steady with a girl. Receiving very little love from either parent, Phil sought fulfillment and acceptance through having these girlfriends. In college, the relationships became sexual. They were never long lasting, usually because they were always so self-serving. Being in his own selfish, little world made Phil oblivious to the fact that these girls were being hurt by his behavior. He was unconcerned, defining his level of manhood by the number of girls he was able to seduce. His sickness was beginning to deepen.

At the age of 20, Phil began dating a Christian girl who gave him an ultimatum: either go to church or the relationship is over. Reluctantly, Phil agreed. Never having an example of a godly life lived out in front of him, Phil naturally perceived God as being an angry judge, waiting to strike him down for the smallest mistake. Therefore, all of his life, Phil's attitude was, "if God is going to get me, I'm going to have fun as long as I can until He destroys me."

One Sunday evening, he went with his girl to a testimonial service, something he had never experienced before. Person after person stood up and shared what it meant to them to have a real and personal relationship with Almighty God. Phil's heart grew harder and more resistant, as these so-called Christians continued to blab their stories of how Christ had affected their lives. (Phil did not trust *anybody* who talked about love or a loving God.) Eventually, a six-year old little girl started to share. Something about the innocence of this precious young life really affected him. He felt his heart becoming softer and his ears more attentive to the message. He knew there was something real about what she was sharing. As he listened to her, something broke inside him. He did not really understand the gospel and knew nothing about repentance. All he knew was that God was calling him into the ministry and that his life was no longer his own.

In the succeeding days, Phil learned more about Christianity and eventually was discipled through The Navigators ministry. His outlook was full of hope, and Phil threw himself into studying the Bible and praying long and hard prayers. The message of the gospel was trying to penetrate his heart, but his perception of God continued to fluctuate. He remembered the brightness of the six-year old girl, testifying about the loving Jesus. But he also remembered his schizophrenic mother, who was completely unreliable and unpredictable. Mustering up all the faith he could did not help Phil grasp a true understanding of God's goodness. Further complicating the problem was his obsessive habit of masturbation, which he could not seem to conquer. He had used it for many years to medicate the pain he felt. Terrified to come out in the open with his struggles, he kept them buried within his own heart, choosing instead to pretend that the problem was not really there.

The relationship with the church girl never really materialized and, with his Christian walk so inconsistent, Phil figured a change was needed. He joined the army! Unfortunately, army-life brought even more opportunities for Phil to feed his flesh. The Bible was put aside and his prayer life came to an abrupt halt, as Phil was introduced to the world of prostitution. And he was ecstatic! He remembered hurting all those girls emotionally in college. But with prostitution, there were no strings attached; the business deal was unemotionally agreed to, payment was made, and his sexual appetite fed for that hour. Phil loved it! Jesus Christ, meanwhile, was forced to delay His work of restoration once again, because of Phil's rebellion.

About that time, he met an army nurse named Liz. Before long, they got serious with each other, and he started feeling real hope about achieving victory in his life. He was getting involved in ministry and would be marrying a woman who really loved God! The masturbation and going to prostitutes stopped; he found his Bible, and his knees started to hit the floor daily in prayer. This was it! Ministry was before him, and the God of the six-year old girl had blessed him with a godly wife. Peace, at last.

Within months, the marriage ceremony was held and the ministry was started. Phil and Liz were one, and his sexual problems seemed to go away. They were living life as any young married couple would. He was sincerely devoted to his wife and to his God, but the matter of the heart and its ongoing wickedness was ignored. He was too excited doing God's work and enjoying the companionship of a wife--who was completely different from his mother--to focus on the black box within, his own heart. Purification was needed, but Phil's head was in the clouds.

A church was planted by Phil and his wife, along with another young ministry couple. It was a joint effort, with the four of them serving as leaders in this new church. Emotions ran high as these young upstarts were all very zealous to blaze a trail for the kingdom of God. The team approach to leadership could have easily worked but, as usual, the enemy slipped in to bring about confusion and division. The honeymoon was brief, as doctrinal differences surfaced within a matter of months. Phil and Liz lost, the other couple seemingly won, and the church sided with the winners. Phil and Liz were excommunicated. The loving God of the six-year old turned right back into the God of the schizophrenic, who was perceived as being unpredictable and unfair. This left him angry and bitter.

After that, he began to drift away from God and away from Liz. It wasn't long before he was knocking on the door of prostitutes again. Things went downhill quickly, and his life sped out of control. Liz finally confronted him one day, and he acknowledged everything. The look of betrayal on her face would be etched in his mind for many years to come. Within a few months, they were divorced.

In the meantime, he switched careers, throwing himself into the accounting profession. Phil possessed the same ability of his father to succeed at whatever he did. Before long, he built up a successful practice as a tax accountant. However, his outward accomplishments only masked the burning lust that consumed his inner life. Making good money simply meant he had more to spend on prostitutes. In a five-year span, he had sex with over a thousand prostitutes. In the midst of his reckless behavior, he incurred over $100,000 in debt to the IRS. Instead of encouraging him to control his behavior, the increasing pressure to pay them back only seemed to drive him deeper into his sin.

It was during this time that he discovered a caring pastor in a local church. One morning he had breakfast with the pastor and shared his struggles. "I don't know what to do, Pastor. I'm tired of failing but I can't seem to stop myself. I have lost all hope and faith."

"Phil, I don't know how to help you, but I am willing to love you where you're at; and I'm willing to stand with you in faith that God will give you the help you need. I will have hope and faith for you. Just keep coming to church until we can find an answer."

Phil tried everything he could think of to overcome habitual sin. He went through "inner healing" counseling. He went through deliverance services. Nothing was changing. He was more hopeless than ever before.

One day several IRS agents came to his accounting firm and carried off his business files. There was nothing left to do but to file for bankruptcy. He was in trouble and did not know where to turn. He felt as though he were sinking into a great abyss. Everything he touched in life seemed to fall apart. He had always prided himself on the abilities he had inherited from his father, but now it seemed as though all was lost.

On Easter morning of 1990, Phil woke up with suicide on his mind. The last thing he wanted to do was to go to church. Nevertheless, he went anyway. It seemed like the longest church service of his life. He left church that morning untouched. The only thing left to do was to go and end it all. As he stood in the parking lot next to his car, finishing a cigarette, a man from the congregation walked past him. Suddenly, the stranger turned around and asked if he could pray with him. Phil had not even responded yet when the man launched into a lengthy prayer, pleading for the Lord's help for him. It was just enough to get him through the day. Two days later he found out about Pure Life Ministries.

It was June of 1990, when Phil showed up at Pure Life. He arrived to find a ministry in its infancy, nothing more than a small house on twelve acres. There was not much there in those days, and people would quickly get frustrated and leave. There were times he would wonder if he would drop out also. The lack of organization could have easily reminded him of his chaotic childhood days. But there were two things very real to Phil: he knew he was in trouble and needed help; and secondly, he knew that God had sent him there. Until the Lord made it clear that he was to leave, he was determined to stick it out no matter what.

Phil had a lack of trust for people and for God. He also felt as though he had gone too far, that he had exhausted God's grace. But as time went on, the Lord began to show him that he could be restored to all that he had once had with God and more. Gradually, his image of the Lord began to change, and he came to realize that He was not an angry tyrant ready to destroy him. He started seeing a loving Father who greatly desired to bless those who would repent of their sin and draw near to Him.

It didn't matter to Phil that the ministry was shaky. He was coming to know the Lord. About half way through the six-month program, something bizarre happened: he was struck down with a strange disease that almost totally incapacitated him. The last three months of the program were seemingly wasted as he struggled with this unusual malady. To make matters worse, the medication he was taking created a physical lethargy that was debilitating. Slowly, by the end of the program, he began to come out of it. But much precious time was lost, and his zeal had greatly diminished. He graduated the program and got a small apartment not too far from the facility. He stayed plugged in, but he was not doing well spiritually.

In the meantime, he had gotten an outside sales position which gave him a lot of freedom--too much freedom. Pretty soon he found himself going into seedy areas of Cincinnati, toying with the idea of picking up a prostitute. He didn't know it, but he was headed for a fork in the road which would determine the direction of his life. For Phil, it was to come in the form of an innocent visit to a female chiropractor. Unbeknownst to him, a battle between the forces of good and evil was taking shape.

During his first visit, he found his mind wandering off to sexual fantasies as the shapely chiropractor manipulated the muscles of his back. He would battle these thoughts off and attempted to maintain a friendly demeanor with her. By the third visit, he had allowed himself to become involved in a personal conversation with her. Things were moving fast, and Phil was overwhelmed by his own emotions. As he got up from the table to leave, she handed him a piece of paper with her home telephone number on it. It was obvious what this meant.

That night, he sat by himself in his little apartment, contemplating the number on his lap. His heart was no longer pounding as it had been when he left her office, clutching the scrap of paper, treating it like precious gold. He was calmer now, but nevertheless, a decision--"the decision"--had to be made. He continued to fix his gaze on the number. His battered heart was torn. His flesh was crying out for a feeding; his spirit was urging a firm denial; Phil saw the two natures fighting within. Eternity was in the balance.

He began thinking about all he had learned in the live-in program. He realized that the decision he was facing was not about whether he would have an affair, but what he would do with the rest of his life. Would he live a half-committed Christian life, toying with sexual sin, or would he begin to see himself as a soldier in the kingdom of God? Something broke inside, and he gave himself to the Lord like never before.

Something was noticeably different about Phil after that. He had an enthusiasm like never before. Instead of putting out the bare minimum of effort spiritually, he was pressing into God with all of his heart. Not long after that, he was asked to run the PLM support group that met in Cincinnati every week. The next Monday evening, while sitting with the men there, the Holy Spirit came upon him and seemed to say, "If you will become an intercessor for these men, I will build in their lives and I will build in your life." Phil really began crying out to God for them.

Realizing how vulnerable he had made himself in his sales position, he began considering a way out of it. It was perfect timing, because PLM desperately needed help. He began fielding the barrage of telephone calls the ministry was receiving from struggling Christians. No one was really dealing with sexual sin in the Church in those days, and the ministry was being inundated with calls from people in need. The problem Phil faced was that the men who could not (or would not) come to the live-in program were without any form of structure. They would call and talk to Phil when things were going poorly, but they did not have the necessary self-discipline to do what they were being instructed to do. Phil was becoming increasingly frustrated, feeling as though he were wasting his time. It was during this time that Phil played such a large part in developing the Overcomers-At-Home program. This is a structured program which enables men and their wives to receive counseling over the telephone.

The new program was made available through the ministry newsletter, and before long, Phil was counseling at least twenty men each week on an ongoing basis. He continued this regiment for the next six months, greatly ministering to many people. Then one day the Lord spoke to him and told him that His restoration process in Phil's life was not yet complete. He wanted him to return home to be restored to his home church and to his ex-wife, who had since become a member there. Phil was stunned but willing to be obedient.

In December of 1991, after a year and a half in Kentucky, he returned to his church, a changed man. The pastors of that church recognized his face, but his spirit and everything else about him was different. God had changed him from the inside out! For the next year, these experienced pastors worked with him diligently. The restoration process was lengthy, but Phil stuck with it. After a year as an understudy, Phil was appointed as an associate pastor there at the church. While all of this was going on, he and Liz were also undergoing a carefully monitored restoration process. Liz needed much healing, and things were handled slowly. On April 24, 1994, the two were remarried. The restoration was now complete.

Since that time, Phil has helped many men in his own area and in 1999, he and Liz made the final payment on the $100,000 debt he had incurred with the Internal Revenue Service. The Overcomers-At-Home Program, which he was so instrumental in creating, continues to flourish as men's lives are changed and marriages are restored.

# 8

# Music on the Altar

"The refining pot is for silver and the furnace for gold, but the LORD tests hearts."

Solomon

Justin Carabello was quickly becoming known in the academic circles of Pennsylvania as one of the most promising band teachers in the state. His band program received statewide recognition as one of the most elite junior high music departments around. In only his third year of teaching, his jazz ensemble was awarded a performance at the Pennsylvania Music Educators Conference--an accomplishment few band leaders ever enjoy. Undoubtedly, he was the rising star of his district.

Little did his superiors know that Justin had become increasingly addicted to sexual sin. Although he was working fourteen to sixteen hour days, he always managed to find the time to go to adult bookstores and massage parlors. The money for all of this came from a petty cash fund he had established specifically for his band. Justin's whole life began unraveling when his wife found out about his secret life and forced him to confess his embezzlement.

Growing up as the son of a church organist meant that Justin was around Christian people all the time. He became increasingly convinced that he could never have any fun in life if he were a Christian and started resenting the way the Bible teaches people to live. This bitterness toward God was as a direct result of being cruelly picked on by other kids in the fifth grade. Because of his soft-spoken nature and his short stature, the other kids would call him "a runt," and ostracize him each day from their games. The situation at school escalated to the point where Justin's parents had to talk with his principal to see if something could be done. This only made matters worse, as the kids teased him and called him a crybaby. Great damage was done--such torment and humiliation would have lasting effects upon this youngster.

His anger was channeled into becoming the best at whatever he did. If it was swimming or tennis or music, Justin was absolutely determined to "give them something to talk about." The world was going to know about Justin Carabello! Others were going to respect him, no matter what it took.

One day, at the age of twelve, he and a couple of his friends stumbled across a *Playboy* magazine. The memory of those pictures lingered in his mind for a long time. It was not possible for him to understand at this young age, how far this sin would take him.

It was also about this time that his parents left their liturgical church in favor of a Pentecostal church. Justin tells of his early experiences:

It wasn't long before I had the whole Christian thing down. I had all the answers in Sunday School, played in the church band, and even sat in the front pew with good old Sister Jackson. I was in church at least three times a week. My pastor was a fiery preacher who did not mince words with his congregation. I knew the truth and that I was headed for the pit of hell if I didn't repent of my sin and start living for Jesus. But I continued to buy into the lie that being a Christian was pure slavery to some puritanical code of oppressive moral laws. None of this was founded upon what I saw from my parents or the other church people. They were always full of the blessed life that comes with being filled with the Holy Spirit. I was simply unwilling to give up the thrill of chasing after sex. And since church attendance was mandatory for members of my family, I simply learned to manufacture the appearance of godliness.

Justin learned early how to play the part of Christianity at home, but the reality was that his life revolved around masturbation and girls. He quickly learned that girls were attracted to boys who seemed to care about them. Justin became a master at playing the part of someone who was sensitive and caring. Finding girls who would buy his phony sincerity was not difficult.

Although he was in trouble spiritually, Justin still excelled in school and was accepted into a prestigious Christian college where he majored in music. It was then that he settled into a pattern of running to his sexual sin whenever he felt lonely, unloved, rejected, or worthless. During the summers, while he was in college, he began to frequent adult bookstores and make visits to strip clubs. It wasn't long before he discovered the underground world of massage parlors and eventually houses of prostitution. He convinced himself that frequenting prostitutes was more noble since he would no longer be victimizing innocent women. A deep craving began to grow within him to intimately know (and have a part in) the underground world of the sex-for-sale industry. The actual sex had long lost its thrill. Now he burned inside with a desire to know as much as he could about the women who were living this deviant lifestyle. He would spend hours planning and choosing just where and with whom he would spend his time. He would make daily calls to find out who was "in," always looking for a new face or someone intriguing. Several times he ended up in relationships with women like this--his ultimate fantasies turning into dark realities. By the time he graduated from college, he was a full-blown sex addict.

Over the next four years, it seemed like outwardly everything went his way. He married a nice girl who was totally committed to their marriage and wanted God at its center. It was then that he became the band director at the affluent, suburban junior high school where he would have such success. Justin's job became his supreme idol, vying only with his secret obsession with sex as the passion of his life. Although he and his wife attended church, Justin had no real interest in what was going on there.

His wife quickly came to realize that she was just not that important to him. Her needs were only important to him to the extent that meeting them would make him feel better. She could not understand why he was always so distant with her. There were times she would beg him, with tear-filled eyes, to tell her what she was doing wrong. She began to feel confused and hopeless. So, when she checked the answering machine messages one day and heard the voice of a female "escort" announce that she was upset that Justin had canceled their appointment, it was not hard for her to decide it was time to leave.

Justin's life quickly fell to pieces after that. He was forced to resign his beloved job when it came out that he had been stealing money. Even though his carefully built career lay in ruins, he still harbored hope of somehow resurrecting it. As he was leaving, his supervisor told him, "We believe you have a lot to offer as a teacher. If you can put this problem behind you, I will give you a reference so that you can go on and have a successful career as a music educator." These words cemented into him the determination to put his sexual addiction problems behind him and to get back to his career as quickly as possible. Not knowing where to go for help, he turned to his pastor for advice, who suggested that he go to Pure Life Ministries. With nothing left to lose, Justin made the ten-hour drive to Kentucky.

Justin knew practically nothing about Pure Life when he arrived. His attitude was that he would do this "six-month thing" (the live-in program) and then assess what else he needed to do in order to put sexual sin behind him. He came unbroken and unrepentant over his sin. He was hardened and bitter towards his wife because she did not stand by him. Even as he was preparing to go, he was involved in an adulterous relationship with the eighteen-year old sister of one of his former students. He drove into PLM as far from God as a person can be.

The first thing his counselor told him to do when he arrived was to establish a daily devotional and prayer time. He told him to pray at least thirty minutes and read two to three chapters of the Bible everyday. He was also expected to do his daily homework in *The Walk of Repentance* (the Bible study curriculum of the live-in program). The hardest thing he was asked to do was to pray for his wife. He wanted to remain cold towards her, but he honored his commitment and reluctantly did what he was told.

At first, Justin approached everything very studiously. His answers to the homework were simply out of the wealth of "head knowledge" he had accumulated over twenty-six years of going to church. His prayers were dry and full of self. He was doing the only thing he knew how to do--fake religion. Then one Sunday morning in a service, after he had been there about three weeks, Jeff Colon, the director of the live-in program, confronted him about being a "Pharisee." He said that if he didn't let God change him, he would never grow close to Him. This was his first true, "rubber-meets-the-road" moment at Pure Life. He knew what Jeff had said was true, so he got alone with God and told Him that he didn't want to be a Pharisee. He sincerely asked Him to show him who he really was and to help him learn to humble himself. God is so faithful! He began to honor Justin's prayer, showing him what Jesus is like through the Scriptures and putting a hunger in him to be more like Him. He slowly started seeing his need to repent and come to the Cross--a place he had always avoided with a passion.

God began to draw Justin very close to Himself. This was a new experience for this young hypocrite! He had never experienced the presence of God like this before. As he began to see what the Lord is like, he also became increasingly aware of how unlike the Lord he had always been. He began to see pride, covetousness, selfishness, and contempt in his actions and words with other people. Many nights he spent out on "the prayer trail" agonizing over his pride and selfishness. Gradually his perspectives about other people began to change. He had always been so wrapped up in himself that he had never had an interest in anybody else. It was like he was coming out of a cocoon and seeing people in a whole new light. For the first time in his life, he sincerely began praying for other people--their problems, needs, and concerns. Sexual sin completely lost its hold on his life as he was changed from the inside out.

Justin Carabello's fork in the road would not revolve around sexual sin, however. He had another idol even bigger: music. His initial plan upon arriving at Pure Life was to complete the program and return to Pennsylvania to resurrect his career. As he drew closer to God, his thoughts became focused on how the Lord could use him as a music teacher. "Perhaps the Lord will have me attend graduate school. Or maybe I can teach music in a Christian school," he dreamed. He thought of every conceivable alternative. He even considered volunteering his talents to help under-privileged children. The painful truth which he did not want to see was that, although he had certainly had a breakthrough, *he* was still in the center of all of his plans.

The real battle in this area began after his first seven weeks in the program. He was finally beginning to establish a meaningful, daily walk with the Lord by this time, and the temptation to begin thinking about what may lie ahead for him began to be almost overwhelming. He started thinking about what he could do for the Lord once he graduated from the live-in program. Being a gifted musician meant that there were unlimited opportunities available. He was anxious to put the Pure Life experience behind him and to get on with his life. And yet, every time he thought in terms of what he wanted to do, he felt a "check in his spirit." The problem was that, in spite of the nagging sense that God had other plans, Justin was determined to regain control of his life. He was more than willing to go "do something for God." There were many possible ways he could work for the kingdom of God and remain.... in control. For the next month, Justin agonized nightly on the ridge behind the office building in prayer, many times to the point of deep sobbing. But these tears were not being shed over a sorrow for his sin, nor were they being spilled for lost souls. The anguish he was experiencing was because it was obvious what God was after--his life. But he was resisting the call. The Lord was calling Justin to sit at His feet, to know Him, and to love Him. But Justin loved his own life more and was not willing to give it up--not even for Him. He describes his struggle:

Eventually I could not set my mind to pray without facing this decision. What was I going to do? Was I going to forsake all and follow Jesus -- not knowing where that was leading me, or was I going to settle for a mediocre relationship with Jesus at best and do what I wanted to do? I knew that, as far as the Christian world was concerned, I was completely justified to think that I could have my cake and eat it too. Yet, at the same time, I was learning to see the hideous sin behind that self-centered way of thinking.

Gradually, the Lord helped me see that there was never going to be true lasting peace in my life until I surrendered what I wanted to do. My all was not yet on the altar. This was so very difficult for me to accept. I so much wanted there to be a compromise--to be able to strike a deal with the Lord. In those times of prayer, I made every conceivable offer to the Lord I could think of. His answer remained the same to all of them, "No, wait. Know Me." I just could not understand how I could be good at something and the Lord not be telling me to go and do something with those abilities. It did not make any sense to my natural, reasoning mind.

God had backed me in a corner and was demanding for me to choose between having Him and having my own life. I remember the evening I made my decision very well. It was a Thursday night, during a meeting at PLM, and the Lord was there in a special way. The meeting ended that particular evening with a staff member encouraging the men to give Jesus everything. He invited the men to come to the altar to pray. I fell in a heap at the foot of the piano and told the Lord He could have everything: my life, my music, my career, my marriage--He could have it all in exchange for Himself. I had never imagined those words would come out of my mouth and that I could really mean such things. I knew that God had finally won my heart. I walked out of that chapel heading down the way of the Cross for the first time in my life. I had laid down my life in this world for Him. Never have I known such peace and satisfaction in making a decision.

Once Justin had allowed Jesus to break through, he began to really fall in love with Him. As he focused on reading through the gospels after that, he would sit in wonder and amazement at the things Jesus said. How had I missed the life in those words all these years, he wondered. He began communing with the Lord in his heart throughout the day. One night, he was laying out under the stars talking to Jesus. At one point in the conversation he rolled over onto his side and the sense that Jesus was right there with him was overwhelming. The innocence of God's love gripped him, making him feel unbelievably pure inside. He melted into a million pieces. He had never experienced feeling anything like this before. His whole desire became to please the Lord in every way.

It became clear to the staff that God was calling Justin to be a part of Pure Life Ministries. In March of 1999, he entered the PLM intern program. He graduated eight months later and was asked to come on staff. Unlike others, Justin was not required to face a fork in the road during his intern program. He had already made his choice, one night "at the foot of the piano." His life was not his own, for he had offered his life on the altar.

# 9

# Out of the Grip of Insanity

"...the hearts of the sons of men are full of evil, and insanity is in their hearts throughout their lives."

Solomon

Being locked away in a mental institution is a very scary thing. Such places are not treatment centers, where *the guest* pays big bucks and the staff tends to be indirect and non-confrontative. No, psychiatric wards can be absolutely horrifying, as only the most severe and extreme cases are sent there. The majority of the patients in state mental hospitals are insane, with their appearance difficult to stomach--their feet shuffling from all the medication pumped into them, their glassy eyes communicating a shattered faith in life, and the smell of their bodies and breath so strong and toxic that maintaining a healthy distance from them is almost necessary. This environment is the scene of countless demonic victories.

Tim Shelby* called Pure Life Ministries from a state mental hospital in New York City. Tim was desperate and in a crisis situation. His most immediate problem was his complete inability to stop exposing himself to women. He was so out of control that, as soon as the psychiatrist would release him from his "locked down" room, Tim would undress at the nearest window and display his "birthday suit" to the city of New York! Even the increase of medication, doubling it from two strong dosages of Thorazine to *four* (hence the name, "the thorazine shuffle"), did not deter him. Tim's sexual addiction had driven him to insanity. Divine intervention was his only hope.

The consensus of the staff was that this twenty-something young man was too far gone for him to be helped at Pure Life. Not only that, he did not even have a relationship with the Lord. And yet, every time they tried to dismiss the idea, it seemed as though God kept prodding them to accept him--in spite of the way things seemed. So, against their better judgment, this unsaved mental patient was accepted into the live-in program during the early months of 1991. Had they known then the problems he would cause, perhaps they would have stuck with their "better judgment!"

Tim's problems with sexual sin began as most do: with masturbation. But because sin is never satisfied, he began looking for other ways to enhance his sexual excitement. He became consumed with the idea of girls seeing him undress. He would wait at his bedroom window, sometimes for hours, hoping that some girls would walk by. He would disrobe in front of the window, acting as though he did not realize anyone could see him. Before long this youthful thrill gave way to drinking alcohol and smoking marijuana. This quickly developed into an uncontrollable habit.

In 1981, at the age of sixteen, Tim was admitted into a drug rehabilitation home for youth. He remained in this clinical atmosphere for the next two years before quitting the program and going back into the drug lifestyle. It was another two years before he was readmitted into the program and was able to quit his habit of drugs once and for all. During this period of his life, his sexual addiction was limited to pornography and masturbation.

Upon completion of the drug program, however, he simply switched addictions and once again became obsessed with sex. Tim started spending entire nights driving around neighborhoods, looking for windows to peek into. He would crawl under bushes or climb on roofs hoping to catch a glimpse of flesh. His old fetish of exposing himself to women also resurfaced. Sometimes he would pull his car alongside a female pedestrian and allow her to see him masturbating. These sordid activities were enhanced with frequent visits to the adult bookstores, prostitutes, massage parlors, and simulated sex shows on 42nd Street in Manhattan. He recounts those dark days of sexual perversion:

> My problems with sexual sin got progressively worse, until I became a slave to my desires. I made serious efforts to stop. Over a period of several years, I went from one type of therapy to another trying to get help, including 12-step groups, therapists, group therapy, psychotherapy, psychiatric day-treatment programs, several different psychotropic medications, a year living in a behavioral-modification program, and four stays in locked psychiatric wards--one being a state mental hospital.
>
> It was during the fourth hospital stay that I found out about Pure Life, so I applied to the program. The biblical approach they spoke of was new to me, but I was willing to try anything. I arrived at the ranch on March 1st, 1991.
>
> I didn't realize it at the time, but I got saved when I came to Pure Life. I realized that because of my perversion I deserved to go to hell (in fact my life *was* a living hell), but I had thought that through my Catholic upbringing, I had a good understanding of God and what He had to offer. I found that I knew little of God.

Tim really took to the program, but he had a lot of problems. He was very confused, easily upset and constantly thinking about sex. At one of the first meetings he attended at Pure Life, he got angry with one of the other men. He left the meeting, running across a field in the pouring rain, crying and screaming at the top of his lungs. Despite his deep-seated troubles, Tim seemed to have a genuine hunger to know God. He was very difficult in those early days, but as he began spending time in prayer and in the Scriptures, a gradual change began to take place within him. As he was forced--for the first time in his life--to take responsibility for his own actions, he started to experience genuine repentance. With this turning away from sin and toward God came an overwhelming sense of hope that he could truly change. Jesus Christ became a reality for him. There was a time earlier in his life when he had purposely taken an overdose of tranquilizers in order to get back into the secure confines of the hospital. Now, the Lord became his refuge.

The greatest obstacle which most men who come into the Pure Life live-in program face is the hardness of heart, firmly established through years of being in unrepentant sin while sitting in church singing hymns and hearing sermons. However, Tim didn't have to overcome such callousness which comes from receiving head knowledge that is never lived out. He had just found God and had the spiritual innocence of a little child. The Word of God was fresh to him.

Another thing he experienced was freedom from sexual sin. For the first time in his life he was experiencing life without the shame of sexual perversion. This went on for two months until one day when he was allowed to go somewhere by himself. It proved to be too much freedom for him at this early stage, and he fell right back into sexual sin. This greatly discouraged him and over the following month, he fell several more times. Despair came over him and he gave up inside. Pretty soon he was packing his bags to leave. He could not be reasoned with. He left to go back to New York. Tim recalls what happened:

> Looking back, I could see that as much as I was trying and doing, I still held on to my own ideas, my own way. I had yet to experience a complete surrender, a reckless abandonment to the Lord. A good example of this reservation was when my own Bible study plans conflicted with some assignments my counselor had

given me. I expected him to work around <u>my</u> plans, rather than submit to his counsel.

When he arrived back in New York, he plunged right back into his sexual sin. For the next month, he sank deeper into the depths of perversion than he ever had before. One night, he picked up a prostitute who bit him and drew blood. He was convinced that she did it on purpose to give him the AIDS virus. Feeling sure he was infected, he contacted Pure Life and asked to come back. The staff was thrilled to have him back.

I believe that God used that incident to enable me to truly surrender all to Him. Throughout the next six months, fearing that I had contracted AIDS made a great impact on my attitude. The Lord used it to help me to find the freedom I had never before had. I rejoiced when I was tested negative for the virus. It is a miracle of God's mercy.

Upon graduating from the program, Tim became a counselor in the live-in program. This arrangement went on happily for several months.

Early in 1992, the producer of the *48 Hours* television show asked if they could film a piece about Pure Life Ministries. They were going to devote one show to the pornography issue in America and wanted to air a segment about those who had been addicted to it. The staff went to prayer about it and felt as though the Lord was in it. Several men, including Tim, were asked if they would be willing to share their testimonies on the show. They all agreed to do so.

Tim continued to grow in the Lord, strengthening his new-found faith. But even after all that he had been through, he still had a major fork in the road awaiting him. In July, the producer, the reporter and the film crew showed up to film their piece. They interviewed the five selected men sitting in a circle. They took some shots of the property and the men eating supper, and then they were gone. The show was due to air in a couple of months.

About two weeks later, Tim mentioned the show to his mother, a highly emotional woman who lived in New York. She was a professional and was absolutely mortified to find out that her son would go on television and expose his secret sin to the entire nation. What would all her friends and business acquaintances think? She was not a Christian and could not comprehend why anybody would air their "dirty laundry" like that. The real issue was obviously her own pride, but what can one expect from someone who has not come to know the Lowly One. She went into a rage and told Tim that he had to get that segment canceled.

This put Tim into a very difficult position. He did the only thing he knew to do: he sided with his mother. The staff understood the dilemma he faced, but they also knew that it was God's will to do this show. It seemed clear that the enemy was using his mother in an attempt to thwart something God was trying to do. There was much more at stake than just a little squabble. Perhaps tens of thousands of men addicted to pornography would be watching that show. Right in the midst of it would be ten minutes of godly testimonies sharing what the Lord can do in a person's life. Tim distanced himself from the rest of the staff. What had once been a close, intimate unity had now been broken. Tim adamantly insisted that he be taken off the show, threatening to sue CBS if he wasn't. The problem was that the main part of the segment was the interview with the five men sitting in a circle. The ministry leaders thought that it would be impossible to cut Tim out and still retain the rest of the piece on Pure Life. They tried to reason with him, but he was unyielding. Fortunately, when the problem was explained to the producer, he was able to have Tim's face blurred during the interview. The show was saved.

The difficulty now was what to do with a staff member who had rebelled against the Lord and the ministry leadership. The close unity and tight fellowship that is so vital in this kind of ministry had been compromised. If he would turn on his brothers and sisters over this incident, how could he be trusted in the future? How could that fellowship be restored when he wouldn't even acknowledge that he had done anything wrong? How would he teach the men he was counseling to submit to his spiritual authority if he wasn't willing to be obedient to his own leaders? Had Tim shown some humility or had been at all remorseful during the incident, things might have ended differently. But instead, he exasperated the situation with his stubborn and belligerent attitude. He was asked to resign his position. The fork Tim faced can be found in the words of Jesus in Luke 14: "If anyone comes to Me, and does not hate his own father and mother and wife and children and brothers and sisters, yes, and even his own life, he cannot be My disciple. Whoever does not carry his own cross and come after Me cannot be My disciple."

When he first left Pure Life, Tim crashed spiritually, immediately returning to his sin. He entered a Teen Challenge program and got himself back on track with the Lord. While he was there, he wrote a letter to the staff of Pure Life asking for forgiveness for what he had done. He said that the Lord had made it clear to him that he had put his family before Him. In other words, *he repented.* Perhaps that is why things went so well for Tim afterwards. Upon completion of the Teen Challenge program, he entered an Assembly of God Bible college. After graduating several years later, he went to work for a Teen Challenge facility and eventually got married. Today, his life is a shining example of what the Lord will do for someone who continues to repent and to seek Him.

Tim was one who did not make it and <u>yet he did</u>. He missed "his fork" at Pure Life, but the events which transpired after his "fall from grace" show that God will continue to try to help even those who have failed miserably. Tim's current work with drug addicts and alcoholics testify to the fact that the Lord is the God of second chances.

# 10

# A Question of Mercy

"They have all turned aside; together they have become corrupt; there is no one who does good, not even one."

David

Jim* had struggled with a serious addiction to pornography for many years. His habit of going to massage parlors and strip bars was completely destroying what most would consider as being a nice American family. When Jim's dark secret finally came to surface, he agreed to seek some kind of help. It was then that he and his wife, Sue,* enrolled in Pure Life's Overcomers-At-Home program. Both of them received biblical counsel weekly over the telephone and teaching materials which would greatly benefit anyone seriously desiring change. However, Jim's participation was only meant to appease his troubled wife and convince her that he was trying without actually moving outside of his comfort zone.

Needless to say, Jim was not serious about wanting to quit his behavior. Consequently, very little changed for him. Before long, Sue's hopes for a real repentance from him were shattered and their lives settled back into a tragic routine of his sin and her pain.

It was years later, as Steve and Kathy Gallagher were on the road preaching at various churches, that they ran into Sue again. One of the churches they spoke at turned out to be her home church. How happy they were to see Sue again, but how grieved they were to discover that Jim had never repented and that she had finally divorced him.

For some months God had been dealing with Sue about going into ministry. The Lord permitted certain unwelcomed circumstances in her life only to draw her closer to Himself. For instance, the house she had rented for ten years was going to be sold, and she was given two months to find another place to live. She could feel the Lord nudging her out of her comfort zone. It was then she applied to become a student at the Brownsville School of Revival. They denied her application, which left her somewhat confused about what God had in store for her.

The Gallaghers were unaware of any of this when they showed up at the church. Sunday morning services were wonderful with a number of people experiencing breakthroughs at the altar. That evening the Gallaghers became engaged in a conversation with Sue, and Steve felt prompted to suggest the possibility of her coming to Pure Life Ministries as an intern. It was agreed by all to commit the possibility to prayer. A couple of weeks later, Sue sensed the Lord say to her, "Why *wouldn't* you go?" Now she knew it was the will of God and immediately called Steve and committed to going through the program.

This was an overwhelming move for a forty-seven year old woman who had lived a stable existence in the same house, same job and same church for over ten years. The greatest challenge would be leaving her two sons who were now in their early twenties. Nevertheless, she was stepping out in faith and very anxious to see where God was leading her.

The staff at Pure Life was very excited to have a solid, seasoned woman come on staff. The Pure Life training program would help her to develop a deeper walk with God and train her in the principles of biblical counseling. She would be the ministry cook while she was in training, but the staff were looking forward to the day when she could begin carrying the overwhelming burden of counseling the wives of men in sexual sin.

After a three month wait, Sue finally arrived. Happy to see her, the other interns quickly gathered around her, helping her to feel at home in her new surroundings. The six new trainees joined the current staff of seven, making a very intimate and happy family. Every morning the small band of thirteen would meet for staff prayer. This intimate time together was a big part of the reason that the staff could exist in unity under the incredible stress that comes with this kind of work. The only way the staff can handle living and working in this intense environment twenty-four hours a day, seven days a week, is being able to abide in the presence of God and to live in humility and unselfishness with each other. One of the main reasons it works is because the staff members make themselves vulnerable to each other, openly confessing faults and repenting in front of each other.

It was into this intense, exciting, and challenging environment that Sue was thrust into. There were many mornings when the Lord would show up during those precious prayer meetings. His awesome presence would fill the room. The effect of His "appearance" would inevitably leave every person undone, weeping at the reality of how much they still needed to grow in their love for God and others. Every person there would spend time in deep repentance--everybody, that is, except Sue, who remained quiet, hidden safely behind her protective walls.

The others were patient with her, knowing her to be a cautious person by nature. Although it made it more difficult for them to be open about their own struggles in front of someone who was unwilling to do the same, they forced themselves to be vulnerable in front of her, hoping it would allay any fears she might have.

Over a period of time it started to become obvious to the staff that her lack of repentance was not out of caution or fear, but simply because she was extremely self-righteous. It did not seem to matter how strong God's presence might be in those morning staff prayertimes or how much repenting might be going on around her, she apparently felt that there was nothing in her life that needed to be changed!

Self-righteousness can be a very subtle and insidious cancer. The underlying inference is that the person is good by nature and can earn a place in heaven through his or her own goodness. This is the attitude which Jesus faced with the Pharisees, who based their entire faith upon their own ability to keep the law--without God's help! Belief in self is at the root of unbelief in God. It was clear that the quiet faith Sue had in her own righteousness affected every area of her life. She mistook her mild and kind nature to mean that she was full of the love of God. She saw herself as being extremely merciful, but at Pure Life Ministries, she came face-to-face with the "fire" of God's mercy, which exposed the shallowness of her mercy for what it really was.

God's mercy always has the eternal good in mind. Humanistic mercy, on the other hand, is sentimental and looks to coddle and pacify the person. It does not think in terms of what is best for that person in the long-run, let alone the eternal. The primary purpose of Pure Life Ministries, which Sue was seeking to become a part of, is to bring the necessary correction into a person's life who has gone out of control. Sometimes this would entail getting strong (not harsh) with one of the men in the program. Whenever this would happen around Sue, one could feel her cringing inside. She could hardly take it! She became very critical of the staff. It did not seem to matter to her that it was the very thing the man needed to keep him from doing something foolish he would greatly regret later. She wanted every-body to be "nice" all the time, no matter what. She failed to notice the genuine love and concern the counselors regularly showed for their men. She quickly forgot the deep intercession they would enter into every morning for their counselees. If a staff member reproved one of the men for any reason, the mild-mannered, peace-at-any-cost, Sue saw it as a lack of mercy. In the fantasy world she lived in, everyone should be happy and pleasant all the time. But those who pour their lives out for men who are in desperate trouble know that this sort of idealistic thinking is very naive. How dangerous and <u>unmerciful</u> it would be to "sugar-coat" truth for men who are destroying themselves! Reality for the sexual addicts who come to the live-in program is that they have not been able to control themselves in the past. In spite of the terrible consequences of devastated loved ones, lost jobs, alienation from God, and so on, when the temptation to sin arises, they have caved in time and time again. They come to Pure Life because they realize they desperately need someone to be strong for them when they are weak.

Had she been a little humbler, she would have realized that she really did not know the first thing about leading men out of life-controlling habits. She could have learned so much, but since she saw herself as more godly than her leaders, she made herself un-teachable. Pride reigned inside this woman who seemed so meek outwardly.

Sue's fork in the road came on a weekend in which the Lord was stressing the need for everyone at the facility to humble them-selves. It came in a series of messages given by a very humble minister entitled *Self Righteousness vs. Lowliness*. There was much brokenness and repentance during those two days. It was apparent to all that God was trying to help people come into a greater humility than they had experienced before. The ministry leadership knew this was going to be a wonderful opportunity for Sue to repent of her self-righteous and critical spirit. They began praying in earnest that she would allow the Lord to break her of the counterfeit mercy she clung to. If she would lay her own goodness down at the altar, she could learn what it means to be a vessel for the mercy which flows from heaven.

It would take a great humbling for Sue to come to grips with the fact that her righteousness was extremely superficial compared to God's; in fact, as Isaiah said, no more than "filthy rags." She would have to come down from her self-exalted position and humble herself to come to the Lord. It would not be on her own merit, but solely by what was purchased for her on Calvary.

At first, it seemed as though something had happened. There was a crack in the wall. But as time went on, it seemed as though she was once again hardening her heart. One morning a couple of weeks later, the staff was again in one of those times of repentance. Around the circle it went, one person after another repenting. When it came to Sue, she whimpered a little, saying, "I just can't do it, Lord. You have to do it for me." Steve's heart sunk when he heard those words. He knew that what she was really saying was that she was not willing to come down to everyone else's level and acknowledge her lack. Her quiet demeanor helped her get along with others, but she was unbroken inside.

The real Sue came out one day, when Steve mentioned to all the staff and interns to be careful not to run their heaters on high when they were not in their rooms. The blood rushed to Sue's head and when Steve left the room she did something very uncharacteristic for her when she blurted out to the other interns, "I'm forty-seven years old. I don't need to be told to turn a heater down!"

The pressure was mounting on Sue. It was not coming from the staff or other interns but from God. He was not willing to allow her to remain in that unbroken, unsubmissive spirit at this ministry. Every day she seemed more miserable. Although Kathy attempted to talk with her on numerous occasions, she would just shut her out, unwilling to make herself vulnerable.

About three months after she had arrived, she suddenly announced one day that she had to leave Pure Life. There was no warning, no notice, no apologies. Apparently her "mercy" did not need to concern itself with the fact that she was leaving the ministry in a difficult predicament without a cook for the men. She also did not seem concerned over the fact that God had clearly shown her that it was His will that she come to Pure Life Ministries as a trainee. The truth was that she just could not take anymore. Her final words to Kathy were, "I have to do what is good for me, Kathy." Yes, Sue, when it comes right down to it, that is the way humanistic mercy always ends up--taking care of "number one."

# 11

# Death in Small Doses

"See, I have set before you today life and prosperity, and death and adversity; in that I command you today to love the LORD your God, to walk in His ways and to keep His commandments and His statutes and His judgments, that you may live... But if your heart turns away and you will not obey, but are drawn away and worship other gods and serve them, I declare to you today that you shall surely perish."

the Lord

George Mooney left the courtroom in a state of utter shock and disbelief. He came in through the front door a free man; an hour later he was walking handcuffed, in a single file line of men heading for jail. This wasn't just any jail. This was the Nassau County house of detention in Long Island, New York, where he had worked as a guard for the previous two years.

The ride from the courthouse in the sheriff's van was along old familiar streets he had known since childhood. This trip down "memory lane" was quite painful. It was amazing how different the large, foreboding building painted with a sickening creme color appeared now that he was to be a resident there for the next year. A wind of hopelessness and deep depression came over him. Tears ran down his face as reality began to set in.

He and the other men were processed in the inmate receiving area. Being strip-searched and examined by former comrades was an extremely humiliating experience for him. But this was only the beginning. As the "fish," the new inmates, were paraded down the dimly lit main corridor, someone recognized him. Out from behind the chain-link fence the "cat-calls" began: "Hey, get a load o' this! It's Officer Mooney! Hey, put him in here with us! We'll take good care of him!" George heard the laughter and jeering all the way down the gray hallway, past the three dorms of pre-sentenced inmates who were awaiting trial (many of them for murder), past the four dorms of men who had already been sentenced to do time at this facility and on past the solitary confinement cell called "the hole," reserved for those inmates who had caused problems.

Mercifully, the correctional officers leading Mooney along didn't heed the requests of the prisoners who would have loved to have had a former guard in the dorm with them. No doubt, he would have been attacked within minutes. Instead, they took their former buddy, who had been an embarrassment to them all, to protective custody. This was a special module of twenty-four, single-man cells for those who would not be considered safe in one of the normal dormitories. Homosexuals, informants, and ex-cops were kept there.

For twenty-three hours a day, George lived in that tiny cell. One hour, every afternoon, he was allowed to go out on the "yard," where he could shoot basketball and lift weights. Other than that brief "recess," most of his time for the next year would be spent sitting or laying on his bunk. This gave him plenty of time to reflect on how he had gotten in such a predicament. He thought back to the time when he was a little boy, being raised by his single mom.

It seemed as though life was always an up-hill battle for George. The low-income housing project where he grew up was more like a ghetto, with gamblers and drug dealers working every neighborhood corner. Most of the tenants were black and their primary aim was to someday make it out of the "Projects."

The only father George ever knew was his mother's steady boyfriend, the father of his brother and sister. It didn't take long before it became painfully evident to him that he was the outcast. Even though his mother tried to reach out to him as a youngster, George turned to drugs and sex to cover the pain he was feeling. He was thirteen, barely a teenager--on the streets of New York.

How he made it through school, no one knows (not even George). He did have an ability to take tests, which baffled his teachers since they never saw him in class. Smoking pot during the day, George only showed up for the tests. In spite of extremely poor attendance, he managed to graduate from high school with a minority scholarship to a respectable university. George was on his way out of the "Hood."

The unexpected pregnancy of his girlfriend quickly shifted the course of George's life from academics to the army, which he joined to support his child. Instead of life improving, he became more heavily involved in drugs and sex. He was transferred to Germany in 1979 at the age of twenty-one; he was then introduced to the world of pornography and prostitution, both of which are legal there. It was while he was there that he began using heroin.

By the time he left the Army in 1982, he had become a full-fledged addict. Out of control, George worked a number of jobs just to support his drug habit. Actually, it was his drug habit that fueled his sexual addiction, as he would buy crack cocaine for the girls in exchange for sexual favors. Back in the old familiar surroundings of New York, George became a point man for many drug deals. He bought crack for the girls and heroin for himself. He lived this way for three more years.

In spite of all of this going on, in 1985, he managed to get hired as a correctional officer for Nassau County. Unfortunately, even this good job did not sufficiently motivate him to get his life straightened out. In 1987, the New York State Police began an investigation on George which resulted in his arrest when he sold heroin and crack cocaine to an undercover agent. Spending a year in the very jail he had previously worked at still did not change his life.

Instead, his life worsened and continued to spiral out of control.

Nothing became too shameless for George. Sometimes he would spend entire nights roaming the Times Square district of Manhattan, bouncing from adult bookstores to strip clubs to massage parlors, in his pursuit of illicit sex. At the same time, his heroin use had increased to an alarming $100-a-day habit. He ended up living on the streets of New York, doing anything he could to survive, including stealing and eating out of garbage cans. Most nights were spent sleeping on a run-down, stolen mattress in a high-rise, outdoor parking garage. Now fully engrossed in the street life, it was not uncommon for George to see friends shot or stabbed. This was New York--the city that never sleeps--and here only the tough survived.

When it seemed as though he could not possibly sink any lower, George ran into an old acquaintance from his teen-aged drug days, Jimmy Jack* Jimmy had gotten wonderfully saved and delivered from drug abuse and now directed a Teen Challenge Drug Rehabilitation Center in Long Island. For the first time in his life, George saw his great need to change. He knew if Jimmy could change, there was hope for him. He entered the Teen Challenge Center in 1990, and graduated the following year. Upon graduation, he became a staff member; however, his problems were far from over.

Although Teen Challenge had helped him overcome his drug habit, he had never dealt with his sexual addiction. While secretly involved with pornography and sometimes even frequenting prostitutes, George's spiritual life ebbed away. He learned how to act spiritual and outwardly to play the role of a godly man. Eventually, his spiritual strength depleted; he began dabbling in drugs once again. Before long he was back out on the streets, taking death in small doses.

For the next five years, George's life was a roller-coaster ride which took him back and forth from the Teen Challenge program to the street life. It was during this time that he contracted the HIV virus. This was a severe blow for the man with the warm personality. Thankfully, in January 1997, Jimmy Jack confronted him and gave

---

* Jimmy, whose story is told in *The God Who Meets Our Needs* (available from PLM), was also Jeff Colon's pastor.

him two options: he could either go to Pure Life Ministries or he could return to the streets. If there was one thing George knew, it was that he had no intention of going to some strange ministry in the "boonies" of Kentucky. He returned to his old stomping grounds-- the streets. Because of his stubbornness, he took the broad path once more.

Finally, after more degradation, the "city slicker" gave up. Almost lifeless, he ran to his pastor in desperation. "Jimmy, I'll do anything. I need help!"

"Are you willing to go to Kentucky, George?" Jimmy asked.

"Yes, I am willing," George mumbled.

In November of 1997, George Mooney drug himself into the Pure Life Ministries live-in program half-dead. Years of drug addiction on the streets of New York, in addition to his being HIV positive, had brought George very close to the point of death. Exhausted by sin, this street-smart New Yorker was at the "end of his rope." Barely willing and barely alive, George showed up grossly underweight. Coming to Pure Life was his last shot at life -- his last opportunity to find Jesus. The staff saw how bleak his situation was and knew nothing short of a miracle was needed to save this poor man.

It was there that he came to discover that his real problem was not drug addiction nor sexual addiction. It was his unwillingness to fully surrender all to God. This came to light in a most unexpected way. George had always been a master at "working the system." He knew how to scheme and connive to get his way. He did this with governmental agencies, and he did it with the various Christian leaders who had tried to help him. Using a bubbly smile and an adorable personality, George always managed to work his angles to get his way. What he did not realize was that God was bringing him to a place in his life where he would have to make a decision about what he wanted. This started to come about as the Lord exposed him for what he really was. As George explains:

> God knew what it would take to finally get my undivided attention, and He brought me to a place where I realized that He was my only hope. While I

was going through the program, I discovered that I had
no love for anybody except myself. I would go to my
counselor and complain about others. I would always
point the finger to expose how "messed up" they were,
not seeing my own arrogant, prideful and critical heart.
I was extremely unmerciful. God started revealing to
me through His word how I was unlike Him. My
outward mask was ripped off and the real me was
exposed, as God started changing my inside world. As
I read verse 7 of the "Love" chapter (I Corinthians 13)
"... love beareth all things...," my heart broke. How
could this King of kings love *me* like this while I was
unwilling to bear anyone who did not meet my stan-
dards? His love was becoming real to me.

God was softening his heart, but George was quickly ap-
proaching his first fork. The state of New York is very liberal in its
benefits for the needy. Kentucky, on the other hand, tends to be more
conservative in that area of politics. Knowing "the system" in New
York, George had arranged to receive an on-going prescription to
help combat the effects of the AIDS virus. He made an attempt to get
this prescription in Kentucky but was unfortunately denied. The
wheels were already turning in his mind as he sought to take matters
into his own hands:

> It was obvious I would have to return to New
> York to get my prescription arranged to be sent to
> Kentucky. I talked it over with Jeff Colon, the director
> of the live-in program. He agreed that it seemed to be
> the only solution to my problem. I would just need to
> clear it with Steve Gallagher. What I didn't tell Jeff,
> and I'm not sure that I was admitting to myself, was
> that my real plan, once I got back to New York, was to
> scheme my way back into Teen Challenge. I wanted
> out of Kentucky in a big way, partially because I was
> used to the city life, and also because all my friends
> were there. But most importantly, it was because God
> was squeezing me at Pure Life and I was looking for a

way of escape--out of the "fire."

After talking with Jeff, I approached Steve one day as he was passing through the men's home. I quickly explained the situation to him, the need to temporarily return to New York to get my medication. I thought it was the obvious thing to do. I was shocked when Steve simply said, "George, you're not going to New York. You've got to trust the Lord." With that simple statement, he just walked out of the room, leaving me there with my mouth hanging open.

My first reaction was anger. "How could he just blow me off like that?! Doesn't he realize it's my life at stake here?" On and on, I railed against him in my mind. I went out to the "prayer trail" to have it out with God. I wasn't used to not getting my way. I finally calmed down and began to pray. All I could hear was his final statement: "You've got to trust the Lord... You've got to trust the Lord." Over and over, it played in my mind. I realized it was God speaking to me. For the first time in my life, I made the decision to trust God rather than my own abilities. "God, You're right. I've always trusted in my abilities to get things done. This time I'm going to give You a chance. I really am going to trust You this time. I can't afford to leave this place without you Lord, so You're going to have to provide for the medication." As I made this resolution to trust God, I was at peace for the first time since I had gotten there.

With that little bit of hope, George made another appointment to go to the welfare department. The day of his appointment, Jeff Colon happened to run into a graduate of the live-in program he had not seen in a couple of years. This guy was also "HIV positive," and told Jeff that he got his medication from the Veterans Hospital in Cincinnati. George also had veteran's privileges. He immediately cancelled his other appointment and went to the VA hospital, where he not only got the medication he needed but also free dental and eye care. The whole incident was a wonderful lesson in trusting God.

With that experience behind him, George began to put his heart into the program. Instead of simply doing the outward things just to be noticed by man, it began to become real to him that the live-in program was a contract between himself and the Lord.

It was easy to understand why the leaders of Teen Challenge had been so willing to put him into leadership positions in the past. (George is very gifted in his abilities to interact with people.) When he graduated from the program, he was invited to enter into the Pure Life intern program. This he did, spending nine more months in training. When one of the Pure Life ministers accepted the call of God to another ministry, George was invited to come on staff as a counselor.

Note: *At Pure Life Ministries, the funnel gets smaller, the fire hotter, the path narrower the further one goes. In the live-in program, men are confronted with what is inside them--many for the first time in their lives. The few who are invited into the intern program find that God uses it to deal with issues which are buried even deeper within the person's heart. The process only intensifies for the one who comes on staff.*

One of the issues that remained buried in George's heart was that now that he was on staff, he could take it easy. He had paid the price. He had gone through the live-in program. He had made it through the intern program. He could enjoy the benefits of being on staff. He knew how to deal with people, and he thought that he could continue to trust in his own abilities with people to get him by. To put it simply, George entered a phase of spiritual laziness. He lost the determination to seek the Lord. He felt that he had arrived and could relax now. Also, buried deep within him was a determination to go back to New York. Once again, the inevitable fork was looming around the corner. This time, the Lord used Rose Colon as a major player in the unfolding drama.

Two things had occurred with Rose which had affected Steve Gallagher personally. One morning, in the staff prayer time, she had confessed to the Lord "what a witch" she could be inside at times. As humble and kind as Rose is, nobody else would ever think of her in that way. Nevertheless, Rose knew what was in her heart, and she did not mind confessing it in front of others. A few days later, she was speaking in a Thursday evening worship service. There was such a tremendous godliness in her voice that everybody was affected.

In the meantime, Steve was feeling a growing sense of conviction that George was backsliding in his heart. A few days later, George was the speaker in a Sunday evening meeting. Everybody enjoys him because he is adorable by nature, but one did not feel the presence of the Lord when he spoke. His words were dead and lifeless.

The next morning, Steve felt led to talk with him. When he asked George how he was doing spiritually he replied confidently, "Good, everything is going fine!"

"George, when Rose Colon describes what she is like on the inside, she calls herself a witch. And yet when she gets up to speak to the men in the meeting, the presence of God fills the place. But when I ask how you are doing, everything is great, and yet when you speak in the meeting, your words are nothing but a lot of hot air!" Steve challenged.

It was easy to see the difference between the two. Rose was living in a sense of her unworthiness before a holy God. George, on the other hand, was full of self-confidence. In his prideful condition, he simply did not feel a great need for God's help in his daily life.

It was no coincidence that this happened just before George's scheduled vacation trip back to New York. It was obvious that he was still hanging on to the hope of moving home. Mercifully, he was brought to another fork in the road.

"George, you need to make a decision. You're going to be gone for a week. During your visit back home, I want you to decide where you want to be. If you want to return to New York, I'll do everything I can to help you get back on staff at Teen Challenge," Steve promised. "But I want to warn you that if you decide you want to stay at Pure Life, God is going to make sure that you go the path of self-denial so that you can serve these men. You have to decide which way you want to go."

He agreed and left the following day for New York. Teen Challenge of Long Island is a wonderful, godly ministry. Jimmy Jack has a great heart for the lost and for those who are bound up in drugs and alcohol. But this is a ministry located in a place of great decadence. If Pure Life Ministries is a hospital located behind the front lines for the wounded, Teen Challenge is located where the bombs are exploding and the bullets flying with no cover in sight. The dissimilar circumstances have brought about a different focus and spiritual atmosphere for each ministry. George would have to decide if he preferred the more "exciting" location in New York, or if he would remain at Pure Life, where God's shining light of truth would continue to pierce and expose his heart.

A week later he returned. "Steve, I realized when I was at Teen Challenge, that I could not make it in that environment. I need to be here, and I'm willing to do whatever the Lord wants me to do to become more like Jesus."

George came to the narrow path and knew that for him, there was no other way to go. He had to pick up his cross to follow Jesus away from the hustle and bustle of life in New York City. Today, George Mooney pours his life out to all those around him. He counsels men weekly, and is a valuable part of the Pure Life team. Despite his ongoing battle with AIDS, George is more than willing each day to surrender his will for the sake of others. And, he actually enjoys fishing and golfing--in Kentucky!

# Addendum

"You are the salt of the earth; but **if** the salt has become tasteless, how will it be made salty again? It is good for nothing anymore, except to be thrown out and trampled under foot by men." (Matthew 5:13)

"For **if** you love those who love you, what reward have you? Do not even the tax-gatherers do the same? And **if** you greet your brothers only, what do you do more than others? Do not even the Gentiles do the same?" (Matthew 5:46-47)

"For **if** you forgive men for their transgressions, your heavenly Father will also forgive you.  But **if** you do not forgive men, then your Father will not forgive your transgressions." (Matthew 6:14-15)

Then Jesus said to His disciples, "**If** anyone wishes to come after Me, let him deny himself, and take up his cross, and follow Me." (Matthew 6:24)

And He said to him, "Why are you asking Me about what is good? There is only One who is good; but **if** you wish to enter into life, keep the commandments." (Matthew 19:17)

Jesus said to him, "**If** you wish to be complete, go and sell your possessions and give to the poor, and you shall have treasure in heaven; and come, follow Me." (Matthew 19:21)

"But **if** that evil slave says in his heart, 'My master is not coming for a long time,' and shall begin to beat his fellow slaves and eat and drink with drunkards; the master of that slave will come on a day when he does not expect him and at an hour which he does not know, and shall cut him in pieces and assign him a place with the hypocrites; weeping shall be there and the gnashing of teeth. (Matthew 24:48-51)

Jesus therefore was saying to those Jews who had believed Him, "**If** you abide in My word, then you are truly disciples of Mine;" (John 8:31)

Jesus said to them, "**If** God were your Father, you would love Me; for I proceeded forth and have come from God, for I have not even come on My own initiative, but He sent Me." (John 8:42)

"Truly, truly, I say to you, **if** anyone keeps My word he shall never see death." (John 8:51)

"I am the door; **if** anyone enters through Me, he shall be saved, and shall go in and out, and find pasture." (John 10:9)

Jesus said to her, "Did I not say to you, **if** you believe, you will see the glory of God?" (John 11:40)

"Truly, truly, I say to you, unless a grain of wheat falls into the earth and dies, it remains by itself alone; but **if** it dies, it bears much fruit." (John 12:24)

"**If** anyone serves Me, let him follow Me; and where I am, there shall My servant also be; **if** anyone serves Me, the Father will honor him." (John 12:26)

"**If** you know these things, you are blessed **if** you do them." (John 13:17)

"By this all men will know that you are My disciples, **if** you have love for one another." (John 13:35)

"**If** you love Me, you will keep My commandments." (John 14:15)

Jesus answered and said to him, "**If** anyone loves Me, he will keep My word; and My Father will love him, and We will come to him, and make Our abode with him." (John 14:23)

"**If** anyone does not abide in Me, he is thrown away as a branch, and dries up; and they gather them, and cast them into the fire, and they are burned. **If** you abide in Me, and My words abide in you, ask whatever you wish, and it shall be done for you." (John 15:6-7)

"**If** you keep My commandments, you will abide in My love; just as I have kept My Father's commandments, and abide in His love." (John 15:10)

"You are My friends, **if** you do what I command you." (John 15:14)

So then, brethren, we are under obligation, not to the flesh, to live according to the flesh-- for **if** you are living according to the flesh, you must die; but **if** by the Spirit you are putting to death the deeds of the body, you will live. (Romans 8:12-13)

that **if** you confess with your mouth Jesus as Lord, and believe in your heart that God raised Him from the dead, you shall be saved; (Romans 10:9)

Behold then the kindness and severity of God; to those who fell, severity, but to you, God's kindness, **if** you continue in His kindness; otherwise you also will be cut off. (Romans 11:22)

**If** any man destroys the temple of God, God will destroy him, for the temple of God is holy, and that is what you are. (I Corinthians 3:17)

but **if** anyone loves God, he is known by Him. (I Corinthians 8:3)

by which also you are saved, **if** you hold fast the word which I preached to you, unless you believed in vain. (I Corinthians 15:2)

Therefore **if** any man is in Christ, he is a new creature; the old things passed away; behold, new things have come. (II Corinthians 5:17)

Test yourselves to see **if** you are in the faith; examine yourselves! Or do you not recognize this about yourselves, that Jesus Christ is in you-- unless indeed you fail the test? (II Corinthians 13:5)

And let us not lose heart in doing good, for in due time we shall reap **if** we do not grow weary. (Galatians 6:9)

yet He has now reconciled you in His fleshly body through death, in order to present you before Him holy and blameless and beyond reproach-- **if** indeed you continue in the faith firmly established and steadfast, and not moved away from the hope of the gospel that you have heard, which was proclaimed in all creation under heaven, and of which I, Paul, was made a minister. (Colossians 1:22-23)

**If** we endure, we shall also reign with Him; **If** we deny Him, He also will deny us;  (II Timothy 2:12)

Therefore, **if** a man cleanses himself from these things, he will be a vessel for honor, sanctified, useful to the Master, prepared for every good work. (II Timothy 2:21)

how shall we escape **if** we neglect so great a salvation? After it was at the first spoken through the Lord, it was confirmed to us by those who heard, (Hebrews 2:3)

but Christ was faithful as a Son over His house whose house we are, **if** we hold fast our confidence and the boast of our hope firm until the end. (Hebrews 3:6)

For we have become partakers of Christ, **if** we hold fast the beginning of our assurance firm until the end;  (Hebrews 3:14)

For **if** we go on sinning willfully after receiving the knowledge of the truth, there no longer remains a sacrifice for sins,  (Hebrews 10:26)

but My righteous one shall live by faith; and **if** he shrinks back, My soul has no pleasure in him.  (Hebrews 10:38)

But **if** you are without discipline, of which all have become partakers, then you are illegitimate children and not sons.  (Hebrews 12:8)

See to it that you do not refuse Him who is speaking. For **if** those did not escape when they refused him who warned them on earth, much less shall we escape who turn away from Him who warns from heaven. (Hebrews 12:25)

**If** anyone thinks himself to be religious, and yet does not bridle his tongue but deceives his own heart, this man's religion is worthless.  (James 1:26)

What use is it, my brethren, **if** a man says he has faith, but he has no works? Can that faith save him?  (James 2:14)

Even so faith, **if** it has no works, is dead, being by itself.  (James 2:17)

For **if** after they have escaped the defilements of the world by the knowledge of the Lord and Savior Jesus Christ, they are again entangled in them and are overcome, the last state has become worse for them than the first. (II Peter 2:20)

**If** we say that we have fellowship with Him and yet walk in the darkness, we lie and do not practice the truth; (I John 1:6)

**If** we confess our sins, He is faithful and righteous to forgive us our sins and to cleanse us from all unrighteousness. (I John 1:9)

And by this we know that we have come to know Him, **if** we keep His commandments. (I John 2:3)

Do not love the world, nor the things in the world. **If** anyone loves the world, the love of the Father is not in him. (I John 2:15)

As for you, let that abide in you which you heard from the beginning. **If** what you heard from the beginning abides in you, you also will abide in the Son and in the Father. (I John 2:24)

No one has beheld God at any time; **if** we love one another, God abides in us, and His love is perfected in us. (I John 4:12)

**If** someone says, "I love God," and hates his brother, he is a liar; for the one who does not love his brother whom he has seen, cannot love God whom he has not seen. (I John 4:20)

'Behold, I stand at the door and knock; **if** anyone hears My voice and opens the door, I will come in to him, and will dine with him, and he with Me. (Revelation 3:20)

And another angel, a third one, followed them, saying with a loud voice, "**If** anyone worships the beast and his image, and receives a mark on his forehead or upon his hand," (Revelation 14:9)

And **if** anyone's name was not found written in the book of life, he was thrown into the lake of fire. (Revelation 20:15)

# Point of Surrender

God, I can't seem to find my way, out of my self and pride
Don't know what to ask, nor pray: full of confusion inside.

I can't believe I'm so blind to selfishness and delusion.
I only think of me and mine, is all that I have just illusion?

Heaven is calling; Hell is raging.  The point of surrender draws near.
My soul is troubled, my mind is racing, my flesh rises up in fear.

I would rather give up or die than face what I really am.
Not sure if it's even possible to find a way out of this jam.

The pressures inside, Lord, are great, to run away from Your light.
Somehow, before it's too late, I must learn to stand up and fight.

Hell is plotting, Heaven is pleading.  The point of surrender has come.
The middle ground is surely fleeting.  Will I give all that I am to the Son?

O Lord, must I face this fork in the way?  Is there no way I can wait?
I wish I'd have more time to play, but I must choose before it's too late.

The crossroad is here, my choices Two;  it's obvious what I must choose.
From now on with self-will I'm through: 'Cause if not it's Jesus I lose.

Heaven rejoices, Hell is vanquished.  The point of surrender is past.
Peace is mine, no more in anguish, self-will is conquered at last.

Rob Nicholson,
Pure Life Ministries